Scarabsistah LLC, Publishing Division
P.O. Box 231313
Detroit, MI 48223-1313
Scarabsistah L.L.C., Publishing Division
Copyright (c) 2003 by Kamilah Hasan
International Standard Book Number:
0-9741309-7-4

Library of Congress Catalog Card Number:
2003092956

Cover Photograph: Ifoma
Illustrations: Jevon Dismuke
Cover Design: Roots Visual Designs, LLC

A Taste Of My Forehead & Backside

VOLUME 1: RELATIONSHIPS

-Kamilah Hasan

Scarabsistah L.L.C., Publishing Division

Prayer

May these written words inspire the divinity in each brother to become God and each sister to become Goddess. May all brothers and sisters receive the gifts of body, mind, spirit, health, love, creativity, and the power of the will to walk by faith in this life's journey. We ask God and the spirit world to bless each reader with divine knowledge and love, as these written words assist them on their path of creativity. **Amen-Aten-Ra**.

Mother Isis-Aten

Dedication

This book is in dedication to the Divine Spirit World and to my dear cousin Kearta, who has joined its magnificence. Though words cannot express my gratitude and appreciation for all that you have given me, I would like to graciously say thank you. Thank you for your guidance, your assistance, your generosity, your love, and your truth. And may all that I do and speak in this lifetime and beyond reflect and revere your beauty, your love, your generosity, and your truth.

Introduction

A Taste of My Forehead and Backside is an adventurous book of poetry. Kamilah Hasan takes you on journeys that are cerebral and funky. Things we know and have experienced, we may experience again through her work. Often the dialect will take us directly to the place she wants us to be. In a time where thinking is not a premium and to stimulate or sexually arouse one seems in many cases to be the only goal for many new writers, Kamilah's work is refreshing, because there is wisdom in her words "It's funny how one's past will re-present itself re-present itself and re-present itself until its purpose has been fulfilled". There is love in her heart "I guess I weaned you to early stop tending to your needs to soon".

Many of her poems tell stories in the fashion of a Paul Laurence Dunbar or a Langston Hughes. She captures the language, the mood and the sassiness of our culture. You can almost see her standing there with hands on hips head tilted to the side and eyes piercing through your soul. Prepare for the journey. Sister Hasan has mapped out an exciting adventure through the treasure chest of her life. I think you will discover her treasures are our pleasures that grace our lives as well.

Abiodun Oyewole
"The Last Poets"

Preface

A few years back, while visiting a friend in New York City, I met a brother that was born and raised in Africa but lived and labored in the big apple as an astrologer and jeweler. He invited my friends and I to dine with him and friends on some delectable African cuisine and stimulating conversation. A thought-provoking topic seemed to surface, which dealt with the art of "Body Reading", a skill his elders passed on to him. My intrigue for the discussion became heightened when he spoke the undeniable truth on my disposition, which he interpreted from select parts of my body. Curiosities beget the questioning of characteristics of other body parts, with the hope of grasping a slight taste of the science. As he graciously expounded on the subject, the elements of forehead and backside were most prominently positioned in my mind. His uncomplicated statement that the size and shape of one's forehead and backside correlates to one's spirit was so profound. *Deeeep*, ...I thought, as I related these particulars to my person, *I've been blessed with a whole lot of spirit!*

This book of poetry was written to give you, the reader, a taste of my spirit. And though I would love to give more, a taste is all that I have, because my spirit is in a continuous evolution through the process of change; the process of life. Change is the only certainty in life; hence in order to live, one has to change. One has to bend with the wind, flow with the waves, accept, and keep on pushing, keep on living, keep on loving and keep on learning. Without labeling, without judgment, without personalizing, without making things more than what they are...experiences. All of life's experiences bring lessons, if learned, can transform into divine blessings; Blessings that can catapult one into a new state of being, so one is able to enjoy the journey of life. "Life is a journey, not a destination". So enjoy your journey; enjoy your experiences; learn their lessons for they are truly gifts wrapped in unique packages. You only need to "change" your perception in order to see and claim them. My hope is that you not only enjoy and claim all the gifts that your journey in this life has and will continue to bring, but that you also enjoy and receive all the gifts that this book of poetry has been designed to bring as well.

This book of poetry shares a taste of my journey, a taste of my personality, my being, my growths, my pains and my triumphs that only the nature of relationships allows one to experience, to imagine, to desire, to reflect....to write. These poems are written and creatively expressed in an insightful (forehead) yet sassy (backside) tone, in hopes to bring humor, to incite and inspire its readers to grow, to triumph, to creatively express and cultivate through all of life's relationships, those experienced, imagined or desired. For it is through the relating with Other, which mirrors what is needed to properly relate with Self. And it is through the proper relationship with Self that brings joy in relating with Other. So on that note....Happy Relations!

May Goodness and Love (Our Divine Creator) guide you along your journey in this lifetime, and beyond.

Peace & Blessings
Milah

A Taste Of My Forehead & Backside

VOLUME 1: RELATIONSHIPS

Table of Contents

VOLUME ONE: RELATIONSHIPS

Forehead 1

Backside 48

Forehead & Backside 83

Forehead

Round and protruding
And intellect that is exuding from
Eyes, lips, and tongue

It was once young
Now growing in Wisdom
Love, Humor and Compassion

For it is on a mission
To be God led
Are you ready for A Taste of My... Forehead?

KEARTA

(August 9, 1979 - July 21, 1995)

I LONG FOR HIM TO ANSWER MY QUESTION
WHY?
WHY SO YOUNG WITH ASPIRATIONS SO HIGH
BUT WHO AM I TO ASK WHY?
SO I MUST BRING MYSELF TO UNDERSTAND

WHY?
BECAUSE YOU BELONG TO HE
THE ALL KNOWING
THE BENEFICENT
THE WISEST OF THE WISE
WHO KNOWS THAT YOUR NEEDED REST
IS MORE IMPORTANT THAN SELF-CENTERED CRIES

AND THOUGH I RECOGNIZE THIS
I STILL DROWN IN PAIN
BECAUSE IT FEELS LIKE I WON'T EVER SEE YOU AGAIN
BUT I SHALL
AND WE SHALL REUNITE WITH SUPREME CELEBRATION!
AND THIS REVELATION
MOVES ME TO LIVE WITH GRATIFICATION AND
ASPIRATION!

SO MY SORROWS TURN TO DELIGHT!
BECAUSE I KNOW WHERE YOU ARE
ABOVE THE HIGH SKIES
SAFE IN THE ARMS OF THE ALMIGHTY
BECAUSE I KNOW WHOM YOU'RE WITH
AND YOU DESERVE THAT PRECIOUS GIFT

SO I WILL LET YOU REST PEACEFULLY
AND I WILL NEVER FORGET THE LOVE
AND THE MANY BEAUTIFUL EXPERIENCES WE SHARED
MY KEETA KUTIE

LOVE YOUR FIRST COUSIN, SISTER, FRIEND

WILL MY BROTHER REGAIN HIS PEACE? ——

GOT DAMN IT!
HE'S BOUT TO DRIVE BACK 'ROUN
I AIN'T RAN NO RED LIGHT
HELL I'VE TURNED DOWN MY SOUNDS
SO WHY HE BOUT TO BOTHER ME?
SIMPLE ANSWER
I'M BLACK
AND HE'S A WHITEE

UM, UM, UMPH...
LOOK HOW MR. TURNER STARIN AT ME
LIKE HE WANNA QUESTION ME ON MY TARDINESS
I'VE BEEN WORKIN HERE FOR SEVENTEEN YEARS
AND I'M STILL GOING THROUGH THIS SIMPLE MESS
FIVE TIMES I'VE BEEN ABSENT IN ALL DEEZ YEARS
AND HE STILL TRYIN TO BRING
MY FAMILY AND I TEARS
BUT AIN'T NONE GONE FALL
CUZ I'M MUCH TOO STRONG
AND I KNOW DAT MY LORD
WILL PUNISH DOSE DAT DO WRONG

HEY BABY!
I'VE HAD A HARD DAY
GOT PULLED OVER BY THE PIGS AND
DEY MADE ME LATE
WELL YEAH BABY...I...I KNOW THAT THE
GAS BILL IS PAST DUE
AND I'M WORKIN ON SUMPTHIN BABY
DAT'LL MAKE THINGS BRAND NEW
YEAH I KNOW I KEEP SAYIN DAT
THINGS WILL BE FINE
I'M WORKIN REAL HARD BABY
JUST GIVE ME SOME MO' TIME

WELL DINNER SMELLS GOOD
WHAT YA DONE COOKED?
NOW WHY YOU GOTTA SAY
ALL I DO IS EAT AND SLEEP?
WHEN I'VE BEEN HUSTLIN ALL DAY
TO PUT MONEY IN YO POCKET BOOK

COME ON NOW BABY
I DON'T WANT TO ARGUE
I'M DOING MY BEST AND
YOU KNOW DIS IS TRUE
CAN'T COME HOME FOR TWO SECONDS WITHOUT YOU
PICKIN ON ME
SO I'LL JUST LEAVE AND HEAD OUT TOWARDS
THE BAR DOWN THE STREET
AND I'LL BE BACK WHEN I COME BACK!
SO DON'T WAIT UP FOR ME

MR. BARTENDER, BARTENDER
PLEASE ...ANOTHER SHOT OF DAT YAK
CUZ WHEN I DECIDE TO GO HOME
I WANNA HEAD STRAIGHT FOR DA SACK
CUZ MY WIFE IS JUST ITCHIN
TO JUMP ON MY BACK
SHE DONE GOT ON MY NERVES
WIT ALL DAT YIP'IDY YACKIN
SHE SHOULD BE HAPPY THAT I'M A GOOD MAN
AND I AIN'T IN TO DAT SMACKIN
SO COME ON MR. BARTENDER
TONIGHT...I DON'T WANT THE DRINKS TO STOP
I WANNA FEEL DAT YAK FLOW DOWN MY CHEST
SMOOTH AND HOT
GONE MAKE ME FEEL A LOT BETTER
SO KEEP SLIDIN ME SHOTS

HEY MR. BARTENDER, TELL ME
WHO'S DAT LADY IN RED, LOOKIN AT ME?
I AIN'T SEEN HER IN HERE BEFOE
IS SHE NEW ON DA STREETS?

SHE KEEP STARIN AT ME WIT DOSE
BEDROOM EYES
OH MAN, NOW SHE STRUTTIN OVER HERE
SHOWIN DEM HONEY BROWN THIGHS

WHY OH WHY, DIS BOUT TO HAPPEN TO ME?
I BETS MAKE SHO DAT SHE SEE
DIS HERE WEDDIN RING
HOPEFULLY IT'LL SETTLE DOWN HER JUICES
CUZ I DON'T KNOW ABOUT MINE
IF YOU KNOW WHAT I MEAN

OH PLEASE LORD
HELP ME TO BE STRONG
I DON'T WANNA TO HURT NOBODY
I DON'T WANNA TO DO MY FAMILY WRONG
ALL DAY LONG I'VE HAD TO
MAINTAIN MY CONTROL
AND I SEE HERE DIS EVENIN
YA STILL TESTIN ME
SO I'M GONE STICK WITH DA SAME ROLE

A BROTHA GOTTA CONSTANTLY STAY ON HIS
P'S & Q'S
CUZ THE DEVIL IS OUT HERE
ALWAYS TRYIN TO BREAK YOU

SO I THINK IT'S TIME FOR ME TO
HEAD ON HOME
WORK DEEZ PROBLEMS OUT WIT MY WIFE
'GARDLESS OF THE FACT SHE NAGS
SHE STILL IS MY LIFE
SO I'LL JUST PRAY FOR MORE UNDERSTANDIN
AND THINGS WILL GET RIGHT

I WILL GET BACK MY PEACE!

Son of A Queen Who Ruled The East

He was born the righteous son of a powerful Queen
Who ruled the East
Until they, with ill intentions
Rode over on their white horses
Covered in white sheets
    Enslaving his mind and weakening his spirit
    To that of a worm
    And this conspiracy traveled throughout his sperm
    Holding firm for centuries to come

So now he's the son of a slave woman
Who fears the sight of her child getting beat
So she instills in him to
Always look down at the Massa's feet
Never look him in the eye
Cuz the Massa's better than you and I
For he has the power to make us cry
By hanging you by yo neck
Then cutting off yo private
For his history is full of violence

    So this son of a frightened slave woman
    Who used to be the son of a powerful Queen

    Mind and spirit weakened to that of a worm
    Now has the courage and strength of a dope fiend

He's the son of a Black woman
Who was able to attend college and receive a
"White folk education"
So now when he looks in the mirror
He sees a duplication
Of a White man with black skin
And his mama stresses to him
"We're not like your kin who lives in the slum
We're better than them because we moved away from
That Black folk way of living

See our toilet is inside our home
And they have to go to an outhouse
They wash up in metal tubs
Ours is ceramic!
We can afford expensive rugs"

    So this son of a bewildered Black woman
    Who used to be the son of a frightened ole slave woman
    And father was the son of a powerful Queen who ruled the East

    Mind and spirit weakened to that of a worm
    Has the courage and strength of a dope fiend
    Is now lost in a false world of dreams

He's the son of a lazy Black woman
Who has been on welfare for fourteen years
Who allows her son to sit at home
Without a job
Along with all five of his kids
Only cuz he's giving her a couple dollar bills
From the sale of drugs
To his own brothers
And she lets him bring home all his lovers
Conceive babies on her bed
His mama so lazy and trife
He all mixed up in the head

So now he truly believes
He's not fashioned to care for any female
Nor work at any job
Well all he ends up being is a lazy slob
To every lady he meets
And could care less whether all his "babies' mamas"
Were to be thrown out on the streets

    So this son of a lazy Black woman

Who use to be the son of a bewildered Black woman
Whose father was the son of a frightened ole slave woman
Grandfather the son of a Queen who ruled the East

Mind and spirit weakened to that of a worm
Has the courage and strength of dope fiend
Lost in a world of false dreams
Now has the ambition of a lazy slob

Throughout history we've been robbed
By our own mothers!
But this does not mean we can't stop the rotation
Of this planned cycle
Developed to cause the destruction
Of a powerful race
Yes it's a chase
And we're running from the devil
Who's digging us a deep grave with his shovel
Filled with Rage, Envy, Jealousy, and Hate
What will be your fate, throughout these judgment days?
Will you be the Black woman
Who continued the cycle of our death?
Or will you be
The powerful Queen who rules the East?

Think about it, MAMA!

HE IS A MAN

DON'T TELL DAT CHILE HE'S A BOY!

BECAUSE HE WILL NEVER UNDERSTAND

THE ROLE OF A MAN

BEFORE HE KNOWS IT

HE HAS THE PHYSIQUE OF A WARRIOR

YET THE MIND OF A CHILD

WHO DEBATES ABOUT HIS ROLE

MADE DIFFICULT FOR HIM TO PERCEIVE

CONDITIONED NOT TO UNDERSTAND

RAISED BY THE NIGGAS IN THE HOOD

TELL DAT MAN WITH THE BODY OF A BOY

THAT HE IS A MAN

THEN BEGIN HIM ON HIS JOURNEY AND TASKS

AS A KING!

Choking Myself

Locking and unlocking
Teasing my heart with
Joyful visions of
The most intimate sharing
Drifting swiftly past my eyes through
Repetitive daydreams and
The unconscious waking, and so
This sharing is never felt
Never experienced

Locking and unlocking
Teasing my spirit with
Fun-filled fantasies of
Mental freedom
Verbalizing through carefree sounds of
"Fuck it"
Whenever my inhibitions try to make themselves known
"Fuck it"
Quenching my thirst
Filling my belly
Yet, I never drink from that cup
I never eat from that plate, and so
I am still thirsty
I am still hungry

Locking and unlocking
Locking and unlocking the heavy chain that
Burdens around my collar like
A gaudy piece of fake jewelry
Unfortunately, complimenting
Every one of my dresses worn

Concealing the most tender regions of my neck
Regions that urge for the soft kisses implanted by
Full lips, attached to
My soul

Locking and unlocking
Locking and unlocking the heavy chain that
Mask wild passions
Bound innate desires
Veils my truth
Which struggle for air
Struggle for life
Struggle to go and do as it please
I can't breathe

I'm gagging
Choking
Asking why
Why am I restrained?
Why am I to suffer?
Hearing no answer

Yet, as my awareness slowly awakens
Slowly walk the path of the links
That form the chain which
Enslaves me
Chokes me

Confusion savagely rapes me
Assaulting my domain
As the gruesome sight of blood
Dripping from self-inflicted pains
Points directly to my hands that
Pulls the chain

I'm choking myself
Teasing myself
Starving my life of life

I am the Massa's overseer!

Remember This...

Though I've made many mistakes
Been easily led astray
Can't find the way back to
My Essence
Remember...I am still God's Child!

Might have forgotten how to nurture
May have ignored your cries for love
Your cries for guidance
Abandoning my gift of healing
Concealing the warmth of my touch
I still gave you all that I had
I gave you all that I knew
Gave you only what I'd given myself
Gave you my burdens
My worries
Gave you my fears, doubts, and insecurities
Gave you all that I saw in me
And though what I gave you may have been
Unsatisfactory
Remember...I am still a Human Being!

And being that I may have
Abused my independent nature by
Hiding my longings for your affection
Falsifying my true need for your protection
Your presence
Just to simply hold your hand
Remember...I am still a Woman!
So...

Before "CHICKEN" enters your rhyme
"BITCH" soothes your tongue
And DEGRADATION plants its seed in your wounded dome
Remember this...
REMEMBER WHERE YOU CAME FROM!

Moon Sun

As SHE nurtures the dark heavens with her
Illuminating grace
Revealing the unknown
HE rests

For HE tills the skies and
Generously provides each day
With his invigorating splendor
Responsibly and wholeheartedly
Sustaining all life
Unconditionally

They work together

SHE, though sometimes unseen,
Is always present
And her presence is always felt as she
Recharge her spirit with his all-giving nature
Patiently awaiting her
Complement's silent request to
Exhaaaale

Anxious to settle his head upon her
Midnight's breast
HE adjourns westward with open arms
Displaying the many gifts of his daily toil
That HE toils for her reverence only

SHE is HIS MOON and
HE is HER SUN

They live happily every after in perfect harmony
With Understanding and
Faithful Love

**Dedicated to the Union of
NaKeya and Adrian Bazemore
May the Creator continue to Bless You with
Peace, Love and Understanding**

13

Mama

Blessings of the Divine gives birth to
The Universe
To perfection
Purity
Nourishment and life

The divine will of the Almighty gives birth to
Ms. Alicia
My universe
My perfection
My nourishment
My life

My mama/his wife
My sister/my brother
His lover
And friend

Through your selflessness and strength
Through your focus and guidance
Through those ATM withdrawals and written checks
Through your beauty and womanliness
Through those 5 feet 9 inches of
Sexy slender legs
Soft earthly skin
Flirtatious smile
Head that always looks towards the heavens
Came my many blessings

Through your relations (smile) came
My Mara
My Dhaf and
Yo Milah
Seeds that will grow only the richest fruits
Seeds that will disperse your wisdom and truth
Amongst the forestry of their lives
Seeds that will sow your beauty and your gifts
Plowed from your field of pride and wit
Determination to achieve it
Birthing this magnificence

The All-giving nature of your womb birthed
My magnificence

When I stare into the eyes of the
Ancient Kemetic statues of our
Ancestral women
I see Alicia Lanette
I see MAMA and I say, Thank you!

His Touch

I seen him, but I didn't see him
My eyes quickly swept across his plain
Trying to ignore the immediate spark that ignited
When mine met with his
In a hopeless attempt to run from this
Familiar feeling, arising in me again
After years of hibernation

So I promptly return to my present conversation
As he patiently stands beside me
Awaiting the opportunity to introduce himself
He then introduced himself
Sending me subtle hints of interest, unspoken
That I continue to ignore
By responding with the habitual
"Hi. How are you? May name is...nice to meet you too."
Then quickly return again to this
Seemingly important conversation
In order to keep from taking notice to his
Piercing stare
Trying to laser beam into my person

So I disregard his attentiveness
Continuing on with my chatter then hurry on my way
Just to find myself reflecting on this
Familiar feeling felt with this
Complete stranger

God gives birth to another day
A new hour of business
Bringing our spirits to cross paths again
And I'm starting to feel this familiar feeling again
Yet still unsure of what it is
So I continue to run from his
Concentrated eyes that attempt to invade me
By shyly turning away
Before they tell me something

I'm forced to acknowledge again
Yet afraid to
So I childishly turn away
And choose not to hear it, see it, nor feel it
Until

His hand touched my waist
His touch placed a spell on me with a
Promise of security
That the width of his arms
Which swallowed me in a hug, pronounced

His touch
His vibration
Flowing from the tips of his fingers to the
Small of my back
Sent messages of passion and pleasure
Sure protection
You see his palms told me
How much he wanted me

Whispering
Let me give you
Let me protect you
Hold you
Make love to you

So I gave him me
I gave him me to hold
To protect
To make love to

I gave him my vulnerability
I gave him all of me because of his
Touch

Perfectly Divine Mates

Out of her primordial waters
He came

He came willing and able
Willing and able to make manifest whatever SHE desires
Making their union higher than any other
They love the many ways they can make each other feel
Uncovering all that is real, they are
Perfectly Divine Mates

Who make the Universe go round
They found
They discover
Their completion
Through the synergy of their
Masculine and feminine energies
Balanced in Harmony
Never forgetting that WE
Always subdue I
So they fly in the cosmos of love
Above all limitations
To be their fate
Perfectly Divine Mates

Who no longer place themselves before each other
Because they love each other
For the reason that they can make each other feel
Real gooood on the inside
Can't run, can't hide
From that tingling sensation
That makes ya head pop off!
Lost in eternal bliss
Sealed with a kiss they are
Perfectly Divine Mates

Who shall still meet with challenges
Obstacles placed for one's spiritual evolution
They will always formulate the correct solution
As they search within
Look deep within their hearts
To the essence of Self

In order to help keep their union intact
They act with selflessness
Unselfishly they pacify
The Ego's desperate attempt to
Always control and fix the situation
That inevitably causes confrontation and
Breed barriers for stagnation
Yet they overcome all hindrances thrown at their relation
So they can cipher on...

While her womb produces conscious daughters reborn
And his seeds grow righteous men
Defeating sin by upholding
Greatness
And from this we receive
Truth and Order
They live the Laws of Maat
Clearing clots that cloud the mind
Enjoying all the time spent together
This very precious, present moment
Stress free!
We have
Perfectly Divine Mates

Who take into their union individual gifts and talents
Strengths and weaknesses
That merge into a journey of one
Towards spiritual growth
May you grow in Peace and Light!
May you grow in Peace and Light!

Dedicated to the Union of
Tene' and William Dismuke-Beaver
May the Creator Continue to Bless You with
Peace, Love and Understanding

A 100% Naturally Grown Love

From birth they were created for each other
Pure Love like a sistah and
Brotha, I just adore the way we love
Because it's Honest, Fun-Loving and Respectful
Like family or a friend
Enjoying the weekends spent
You know that weekend we spent...it was so...
Natural!
Like 100% Organically Grown
No additives or preservatives
Because the way we give
Manifest that we live
Happily Ever After!

Immediately after their first encounter at the
Most Romantic Celebration
Black Bike Week (smile)!
She knew they would meet again

Gemini Twins
Both switching to their second personalities while
Momentarily switching back to the first
However, understanding bursts!
Allowing them to maneuver through the moods
No matter the mood
His chivalry has a Grand Entrance at every occasion
They are Reflections
Reflecting each other's strengths and weaknesses

She could tell by his
Touch
That he was a good person
Especially the way he slow-jammed with that sheet to
"In Between The Sheets"
She knew they would keep a love so fun and
Spiritually great
That would make it
Full of flavor!
Like 100% fruit juice
From the juices of fruits that fall from
The Tree of Love and Life
Now Husband and Wife
Sistah and Brotha
Future Father and Mother
Who will continue to show the world
How to love
Naturally

No additives or preservatives
Just United With
Peace and Understanding
Thus creating a
100% Naturally Grown Love

Dedicated to the Union of
Dantaya & Roderick Williams
May the Creator Continue to Bless You with
Peace, Love and Understanding

Mara Netta

March 14th of 75!
She graced our lives
She graced our souls with her presence

Dispersing amidst the heavenly skies
Sweet sounds of silence
A quiet calmness
Inborn obedience
Subtle breath of fresh air
Bringing peace of mind and joy to a new mother
Pride to a father
Harmony to a brother
And we'll talk about what she brought her sistah later (smile)

Ms. Mara Netta refused to let the
Dreadful stories of all the struggles to come
To prevent her from
Becoming what she had always dreamt to be
You see... "M.D."
Ain't no surprise to me
March 14th of 75 she blessed our beings
By being a model of
Triumph!

Sowing the earth with a deep bass line of hard work
Making feet tap and hips rock with
Endurance
Perseverance
An exerting mind
Toiling hands and
One mustn't forget those shoulders
Oh those shoulders!
Which have carried mountains of books
Since eight years of age
While I stood back and gazed in amazement
At her strength
Her drive
The determination within her eyes
Always placing her studies as top priority
All the while I'm thinking, "How does she... do it?"

And she did it!

You see Ms. Mara Netta
Didn't let the
Drama
Keep her from pushing
For her passion is too great
Her passion to achieve
Her passion to succeed
Her passion to stand tall and win
And when this sistah has a passion to win
Don't let the smooth and silent taste fool ya
You bets believe she gets the last word
Even if it takes til 12 o'clock in the morning
On a school night!
Mara ended any and all verbal fights with sis
I'm talking bout going back and forth with
"You make me sick"
"You make ME sick"
"You make me sick"
"You make ME sick"
...I give up!

Mara Netta you make me stick to
Carrying out all my dreams and goals
For you set the stepping-stone for your siblings to rise
You have always been a visual guide
Teaching us by example
Creating in us an ample desire to be as
Strong-willed as you

For you have always been a mentor
A Sister and
A friend to me and
You can always count on me and
Call on me and
Ask of me
For I infinitely, have your back
No matter how childish we may still sometimes act
Our bond is intact
Inbred in our bones
My home is your home
My blood is your blood
Because I love me some
Mara Netta!

23

The Present of the Past

It's funny how one's past will re-present itself
Re-present itself and re-present itself, until
Its purpose has been fulfilled

Fulfilling its purpose
Traveling along the infinite paths of Evolution
While we mistakenly think a conclusion has been met
When yet, it has only just begun!

It's funny how one's past will re-present itself
Stimulating confusion and possible illusions
Thoughts of, "I can't believe this is real!"
"I can't believe we've crossed paths again!" and
"Why have we crossed paths... again?"

It's funny how one's past will re-present itself
Creating stories of irony
Inevitably calculating to
We
For one's progression into life's deeper meaning
Meaning this new life is about to get reeeal...
Deep!

So deep that the hand which holds the TV remote
Will be irrelevant
Or whether German chocolate dessert is his
"Most" favorite
Will only weigh a little bit
Compared to the magnificence of the big picture
The Grand Story behind your union
Or should I say, re-union

Reuniting families previously separated from
Life's busy schedule
Reuniting fond memories of yesterday
Making today even more special

You see the Cosmos had already prepared its potion
Moments ago
Bringing you to surrender
Right on time
It had nothing to do with the functioning of the mind
Our Creator's ever presence had to shine
Making way for Divine Order to lead
Not giving you what you want but what you need
Sending him, sending her
To please
Your Soul's innermost desire to know God
To know Self
To know your God Self
Through the vehicle of love for each other
Through the vehicle of "unconditional" love for each other
By becoming aware of each other
By seeing each other as grand expressions of the
Most High!

Lie on the warm beaches of your heart's yearning
Swim in the cleansing waters of profound learning
Walk the spiritual paths of this life's journeying

Holding hands
Holding hearts
Merging souls
Purging old
Praising Newness
In whatever you want to create and bless
With your Oneness
Your Togetherness
Your Gift

Your present that your past has re-presented you with
NOW!

**Dedicated to the Union of
Shirley and Michael Ratliff
May the Creator Continue to Bless You with
Love, Peace and Understanding**

Pink Nose White Mouth

My friend, roommate, and dearest companion

Your presence has made my
Aloneness
More pleasant
As you anxiously greet my solitude at the front door
You are more than what simple eyes see
A "pet" is a mere understatement to me
For I catch sight of your great spirit
Staring through those
Big pretty yellow eyes
That dilates to complete blackness
Windowing your truth

I've come to recognize why some dislike you and your
Feline grace
That they mislabel "sneaky"
Removing you from God's embrace
For they fail to see that
All creatures are divinely shaped
Which creates phobias in
Sharing the same space
With your mysterious ancient spirit
Many are afraid to come near it
For your vibration is profound
It has walked along the great sands of Egypt
Revered by our Ancestors
Impressed on commanding monuments and
Majestic statues
And so you
Are surely with no doubt
A most treasured friend
With a pink nose, white mouth

Dedicated to My Feline Friend
"Trouble"

A Brand New Baby?

Do you really think that they are
Brand new?
Barely turning three years old
Acting like they're fifty-two
Some of these five-year-olds
Are more aware than you!

For they are old ancient spirits
Who have simply chosen to reincarnate
Through your sacred womb
That cosmic portal that all souls must enter
To be reborn
If one desire to learn their lessons
In order to progress
Yet we keep underestimating their consciousness
Thinking, "they're just a baby" and
"They don't understand, they don't know"
And so you expose them to "bad" habits
Then wonder where they have learned theirs
Mistaking them as being unaware of
What is said and done
But we must watch what we say and do
For they are extremely sensitive to their surroundings
Therefore, it is important that we surround them with
Peace and love
So they can become
Peaceful and loving
Rising to their true state of being
Therefore, we can't continue treating them as
Dolls
As if they were solely created to be accentuated with
"Name brand" shoes and/or clothes
Talking 'bout "I want a boy so I can corn roll...his hair"
How dare we look at these ancient souls as such

Guiding their spirit takes much more than

27

Plopping them in front of the television or
Spoiling them with perishable gifts
In an attempt to compensate for
The lack of time given
The lack of love
Rearing them the exact way your Mama reared you
When they are extensions of you and
Those who came before
Therefore, they should be guided to
Become greater
Giving them more than what money can buy
Not anything less

And I can't help but to express this truth
Because if we continue not to take heed
In the importance of cultivating our seeds
We will surely meet doom
 We must stop polluting our wombs with poisons
Drugs, toxic foods, and hate-filled thoughts
Thinking that it's not going to affect their growth
Or should I say
Not caring whether it will affect their growth

But given that you fill your own temple with this mess
I guess one cannot expect you to
Treat that which comes from you any different
When you're unmindful that
You are both one in the same

One must gain more wisdom and insight into
The higher purpose and role of
Guiding a spirit
Before being so quick in desire to birth one
Simply using it as a means to
Satisfy a need for love
To satisfy a need to love
When one hasn't mastered the love of self

Birthing a spirit isn't going to automatically help
Bring more happiness in your life
Especially when you're not trying to become
Happy within

Education starts at the point of conception
So we must cease underestimating
Who and what these "babies" are
We must cease ignoring their spirits
That embody within
Originating from far-away lands and
Far-away times
We must give them a fair start in this lifetime
By no longer force feeding their minds with
Superficial, Man-made untruths
For they are old ancient spirits
Ain't nothing brand new!

If

If we're afraid of losing each other, from the start
We will never
Re-begin
Remember
Nor return, to Love

Some Don't...But You Gots To Anyway

Some don't want to see you rid yourself of self-hate
     But you gots to rid yourself of self-hate anyway
Because some don't want to see you prosper
     But you gots to prosper anyway

Some don't want to see you rid yourself of anger and pettiness
     But you gots to rid yourself of anger and pettiness anyway
Because some don't want to see you happy
     But you gots to be happy anyway

Some don't want to see you love, live healthy, and feel youthful
     But you gots to love, live healthy, and feel youthful anyway
Because some don't want to see you shine
     But you gots to shine anyway

Some don't want to see you be just and at peace
     But you gots to be just and at peace anyway
Because some don't want to see you rise
     But you gots to rise anyway

Some don't want to see you let the Divine Spirit lead
     But you gots to let the Divine Spirit lead anyway
Because some don't want to see you become, who and what you are
     But you gots to become, who and what you are anyway

For this is what you were created to be and do
And so you gots to be and do it, anyway!

Misery May Love Company But...

Some people have chosen misery
For the reason that
It may be all that they have known
Unconsciously becoming their comfort zone
And out of their fear of being alone
In their death
It creates a strong desire in them to project
Their misery upon you

And so they deliberately abuse, misuse, and
Try to find ways to inflict pain
They craft rumors
Attaching negative words to your name
Lying, cheating, stealing, murdering, raping
In hopes to gain some type of pleasure
Since their life is without
And so now their life is all about
Seeing you suffer
Seeing you hurt
Ignorant to Karma
Ignorant to the fact that
They are only hurting themselves
Blocking their blessings
But nevertheless, you mustn't let them
Take your joy
By allowing anger and vengeance to take residence
In your sacred space
Your sacred temple
Your divine
Your spirit, body, or mind
Because it would give them exactly what they want
Companionship in their misery

So you mustn't let their negativity
Affect you and your rise to Christ

If you reacted with the same stress and strife
It would only show them that their way is right
And it's okay to have hate
Therefore, you can't take their actions personally
For they have nothing to do with you
It is merely their inner chaos projected outward to
Whoever is there to accept
So don't accept anger
Don't allow bitterness to
Enter through your holy doors
For their misery may love company but...
That don't mean you make it yours

I Forgive You

Why is it so hard to do when
It is so desperately needed?

Hanging on to old hurts ain't nothing but
A heart attack waiting to happen
What ever happened to unconditional love?
Everyone has forgotten how to love
We haven't been re-taught how to love
As I justify not loving you, liking you anymore
As I justify not giving you any care or concern
Anymore

Yet I'm starting to think that
Maybe my resentment toward you
And the negative feelings I've held against you
Justified by the "bad"
I believe you to have done to me
Ain't hurtin nobody but
Myself
So in forgiving you
I would be forgiving myself
I would be freeing myself from
The resentment and pains
I've kept hidden within

As I journey towards
Perfecting self
I am being faced with the reality that
I must forgive others of their wrong
In order to forgive myself of mine
So that God can shine through
I have to let go of what my mind keep trying to hold on to
So in letting go...I forgive you
And hope that you forgive me
For any wrongdoings or pains
That I have made and or held against you
For it was not my intent
It was out of pure ignorance
A temporary blindness of not seeing
The God in you
Regardless of what you do or have done
Because I now know that we are all born from
God's grace

I hope that you find it in your heart to place
My deepest and sincerest apologies there
Forgiving me
As I forgive you

To all those persons (regardless of race, age, or creed, whether family, friend, stranger, neighbor, co-worker, etc.) where we have experienced unpleasant events, no matter if it occurred during my very beginnings as a young girl or into adulthood, no matter how small or large our issue may have been, I ask for your forgiveness for any and all the wrongs that I may have caused or have held against you. Forgiving me as I forgive you.

My Dear Sweet Son

I haven't heard your cries for a long time now
I have been deaf to my own
Unable to neither hear nor see
The pains that you have suffered

A thick heavy veil layered upon my eyes
After every beating
Hanging
Rape and
Molestation
Blinding me
Numbing me
To your beatings
Your rapes and
Your molestations

Which took your manhood into oblivion
Not knowing what the experience meant for you
Not knowing what it made you
What you are now
Mama, what am I now?
What am I supposed to be now?
How am I supposed to think and feel now?
You ask
And I don't answer
Because I don't have one
And so I don't want to talk about it right now
And so right now becomes
Never
Never speaking on it
Hoping that my silence would
Make it go away
Not knowing that the experience was
Growing ever so great in you with
More questions
More confusion
More ill feelings
More not knowing what to do
Not knowing what you are

For the veil had become so heavy and thick that
I had forgotten the truth
Mama couldn't answer your question
Mama couldn't end the chaos that ran rampant in your mind
Because Mama didn't know
And how can a Mama not know?

How can a Mama consider herself a Mama
If she doesn't have the answer?
If she can't heal the pain

So Mama covered the pain with
Southern hymns and
Church on Sundays and
You gots to stop cryin and be strong now!
We got greater worries
We ain't got food on our table or clothes on our back
So alls I can tell you is
Just pray
Just keep praying to the Lord and
He'll give you an answer
He'll heal your pain
For he is your only savior

But you never got that answer
You never heard the answer
Because your mind was filled with
Chaotic thoughts
As my mind became engulfed with them as well
And so Mama couldn't hear your pain

Your pains of rape
Molestation
That inevitably turned into
An unhealthy sexuality
Passing through lifetimes
Conspired to pass through lifetimes
And so now you think that you were born that way
Not knowing what to be or how to feel
And since it's

Not okay
For a man to cry
Unexpressed pains and confusion
Turn bright skies dark
Because no one cares about the heart
Of a Black Man

Even Mama has become hardened
Even sister has become hardened
Giving you zero empathy
No insight into the root of your pain
No attempt to help heal it
She only gives you judgment
She only gives you condemnation
Mama, don't even open her arms to you anymore
She don't even reach out her hands to you anymore
And so how can she possibly tell you the divine truth
How can she give the divine answer

My Dear Sweet Son

Your experiences
Your rapes
Your molestations
Have nothing to do with who you are
It doesn't change a thing, my Black Man
My Son
My Brother
You are still who you are and will always be...
God, Perfection, Beauty, Strength, and Love
My Warrior
My Shinning Star
So keep shining, star
Know this always, for it will take you farther
Than what minds can conceive
Forgive Mama
For she has been deceived
Made to forget how to love
How to nurture you
How to heal you
Show you

Teach you what a man is and does
Teach you how a man lives and loves
And how Man's spirit is untouched by
Any experience that happens within this physical plain
For the Spirit holds domain over the body
So there is nothing that can be taken away from you
Your being is whole and enough
Always

So I now make this promise to you in my remembrance
My awareness of this past error
That has passed through our genetic codes
Causing repeated episodes
Causing Mama to become blind and deaf to your pains
I now make this promise to you
In awareness
That I will no longer ignore your pains
My arms open wide to you always
My hand reaches out for you always
I am here to nurture and heal you always
I love you unconditionally always
And I will no longer let selfishness keep me from
Acknowledging your pain
Understanding your pain
Healing your pain
Seeing your divine spirit
Seeing your truth
Who and what you are now and forever
God, Perfection, Beauty, Strength, and Love
My Warrior
My Shining Star

My Dear Sweet Son

My Earth

As I look out over her vast fields of
Beauteous valleys, lakes, and
Mountaintops
I am urged to fill her boundless crops with
Strong righteous seeds
For I know that whatever I sow in
She
I shall reap
Therefore, I keep her fertile Earth
Cared for and protected by
My skillful hands
Her harvest is grand!
For it gives me nourishment
For she gives me
Life!

Saleem

One of peace
Created to never let the
Worldly games and
Superficial
Knock you from your center
In life there will be many splinters
That will attempt to slow you down and
Keep you from fulfilling your purpose

Yet nevertheless, you must know this always
The Creator forever guides you within
Just listen and
Pay attention to
The celestial voice within
And you'll always make the right choice
Thus, never be afraid to choose
Life is about experience
So you can never make the wrong move
Just learn from all the obstacles presented on your path
Then you won't have to experience them again
Make "Faith" your best friend
Moving you along your journey
Returning home
Back to your God self
I am here to help you, always

Open and feed your mind
Greater truths
Setting it free from the shackles of this
Material
And all its grand illusions
Bringing you liberation
Real beauty and grace
Truth and order
Balance and harmony
Know that with generosity
Comes abundance
And prosperity is our birthright
For we are all divinely born

So keep in your awareness that you are
Divine
Always make time for Self

Meditate
Reflect
Breathe
Search within for the answers you seek
Always speak kind and uplifting words
Think positive and healthy thoughts
And don't get caught up in negativity
That may attempt to surround you
Surround and fill yourself with vibrant energy
That will assist you in rising to the God you are
And no matter my location, I am never far
I am in your blood
My love is in the air that you breathe
We are related cosmically
And I don't care how much taller you are than me
Or how much stronger you may be
Big Sis can always take you down (smile)
Though I never would
Because up is where I want you to soar
For I want your life to be filled with
All your heart's desires
And I said "heart"...not mind
May you find and rediscover you in this lifetime
Love your sister, your friend

Your "Mate'y Boo"!

My Beautiful Old Man

My old man...he ain't old
For his spirit and soul exudes youth
I just call him "old man" because I think it's cute
And fun
Since I now can call him whatever I choose
Because back in the day I wouldn't dare attempt to
Call him anything but
"Yes sir" and "Dad"

As a child he had a stern nature and was very strict
I would find myself writing in my diary
"He makes me sick!"
But when I became a young adult
I realized that it was his sternness
Balanced with Mama's compassion
That made me stick to what was right

The only time he would whip my hands was when
My siblings and I would fight, which
He took no mercy with
Because he said that we were more connected than
He and mom
For we had the same blood running through our arms
Through our entire body
And he didn't tolerate any
Disrespect
And for this My Beautiful Old Man
I respect you greatly

I know that you wish you'd done some things differently
And if you could go back and change them, you would
But holding on to the past doesn't bring any good
It only enslaves you
Dad, I am so happy for being a part of you and
You I
I am thankful for inheriting your humor
Your love for humanity
Your love for knowledge
Though I would have tweaked the

Massive head I was given to hold it in (smile)

And you know that tendency of preach'in
I also inherited from you
I've been blessed to be able to
Transform it into
Poetry
Most of the time
'Cause a sistah can still get to preach'in (smile)
But it's all good
Because it is all in love
And I love you always
Unconditionally
My Beautiful Old Man

Re-Latch On To Me

I guess I weaned you too early
Stopped tending to your needs too soon
Your need for guidance
Your need for direction
Your need for my
Unconditional love and
Therapeutic touch

I failed to pay attention
Out of a temporary loss of sight
Out of ignorance
An unawareness of the infinite call for
My healing
My nurturance
And not that overly pacifying nurturance of a
Crippling love that
Inhibits growth
Spoils rotten and
Makes weak
I'm talkin bout a divine nurture that teach
Brotha, how to be a Man
I now over stand that
Your cultivation begins with
My hands
At my feet
Flowing from my breast
Fed with my milk
Formulated to arouse brain cells
Metamorphosing young Black males into
Gods

I am the Goddess that you must feed from
Be nurtured by
And make reverence to
Infinitely
And so the time for you to re-latch on to me
Is now!

LOVE IS

Love is...NOT POSSESSIVE
It doesn't bind
Hinder
Nor attempt to control
Love is...NOT JUDGMENTAL
It doesn't label
Nor condemn
Love is...NOT CONDITIONAL
It has zero stipulations
No specifications and
It is not demanding
Love is...NOT PAINFUL
It's oblivious to harm
And it knows no sorrow
Love is...NOT DECEPTIVE
It holds no secrets
And tells no lies
Love is...NOT FEARFUL
It has no insecurities
It knows no worry
And so it does not hesitate
Love is... NOT SELFISH
It is not egotistical
Nor inconsiderate
Love is...NOT WEAK
It doesn't tire
And it is never unsteady

LOVE IS LOVING

LOVE IS FREEDOM
    It is liberating
    It is light
LOVE IS JUST
    It is equal
    It is balanced
LOVE IS UNCONDITIONAL
    It is understanding and forgiving
    It is compassion
LOVE IS JOYOUS
    It is peace
    It is blessings
LOVE IS TRUTH
    It is honest and correct
    It is righteous
LOVE IS BRAVE
    It is faithful and unconcerned
    It is ready to enter the unknown
LOVE IS GENEROUS
    It is selfless
    It is abundant
LOVE IS STRONG
    It is healthy and it is stable
    It perseveres for it is always able

LOVE IS LOVING
To all it knows
To all it meets

Have you ever met...LOVE?

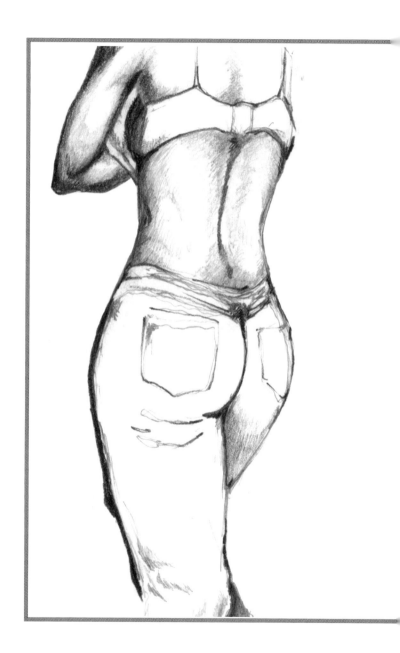

Backside

Round and protruding
A sassiness that is exuding from
Hips, waist, and thighs

It was once slender
Now it is wide
As it moves in a graceful stride
Or strong pursuit
Many salute its power
For it can be fierce
As it pierces its way through
And never subsides

Are you ready for A Taste of My... Backside??

Don't No Bullshit Multiply

I've got two titties
    For two hands
Not a nipple mo'!
    What, yawl all tryin to wear me out?
Den call me a hoe!
    When I'm only giving you what you asked me fo'
Then preachin you can't find no Queen
    When you're helpin me become that
Dick fiend
    Know what I mean?

But nawl, you can't see that
    Don't wanna see that
Cuz all you can see is dat
    Kitty, Kitty, Kat
Ya starting to act and smell like that
    Like a Big Buh'dussy!
Hey I'm just calling you out like you do me

Bragging cuz I licked you down
    Though you looked like a clown, wit yo pants down
I still gave you some
    And I might be Blind, Deaf, and Dumb
But you're Blind, Deaf, and Dumber
    Like a cucumber

Cuz you suppose to be the King
    Guiding and protecting me
But all you worried 'bout
    Is sliding and injecting me
With those filthy seeds
    That ain't growing nothing but weeds

We better do something NOW before we die
Cuz don't no BULLSHIT multiply
We better do something NOW before we die
Cuz don't no BULLSHIT multiply

So when you gone stop blaming me
    For your actions
And start helping me cuz I'm lacking
    The strength to fix this situation on my own
Hell we need two domes
    Infinity/Spirituality
Two Healthy Mentalities,
    Two Powerful You & Me's
So be my King
    And let's use yo ding-a-ling right!
And produce some mo' Queens

Because if we don't we'll die
Cuz don't no BULLSHIT multiply

So if you continue to degrade me on TV
    The more whorish, freakish, and sluttish
I'm gone be
    If you continue to dogg me in your rhymes
Our seeds will mimic this action throughout time

See what you must understand is
    I'm your MAMA
I'm your SISTER
    And your DAUGHTER
And if you keep on
    We shall be slaughtered
Like swine throughout the Holidays
    We are coming close to the Day

We better do something NOW before we die
Cuz don't no BULLSHIT multiply
We better do something NOW before we die
Cuz don't no BULLSHIT multiply

Longing

Another night my heart skips a beat
A beat filled with a hypnotic baseline
Taking my consciousness to the cosmos
As Heaven's chorus travel up the scales
To a high that opens my
Crown chakra
To a truth that only your love can tell

Another night my heart craves
My lips hunger
My body suffers from
The absence of your presence
Your tender
Your affection
Why are my desires left to decay by the hands of
Desolation

Nothing in this world can survive without the love of another
Where are you my Soul Brother?

I'm not that sistah infatuated in being an
Independent woman
I need your love fa'sho!
And just don't know how satisfied you'd feel
Embracing the love of this real
Queen
Just bring your mind, body, and soul
So I can bestow the pleasures of my love hole
My love haven
Which longs to rapture you with

Feelings of completeness
Fullness
Ignited by the perfect warmth that
My flames
Are ready to give you

I can't take lying next to the
Cold crisp air
An empty space
Please relieve my heart from this ache
It craves to wake from the slumbers of
Loneliness
By the willfulness of your hands
Your passions
Your touch
Heals my despair

If my soft supple skin is forced to lie bare
Another night
Without your body's allure
A dark heavy storm shall brew forth
At the crevice of my eyes
Bringing my unborn babies to cry
Rivers
And all sprouted life shall wither away
I cannot go on another day
I cannot
Go on
Any longer
The pains of my hunger

Grows stronger
Each moment that you're away
Please come and lay with my soul
And keep me from being deprived of life

Please come and lay with my soul
And keep me from being deprived of life

This Shit Is Getting On My Got Damn Nerves ———

You know this shit is getting on my got damn nerves
Frying my brain with this
Hurry and capitalize on this thang called
Romance
Contemplating on whether to give him
A chance
When I know he full of shit
Shit!

I'm tired and sick of my
Self-pitying romantic infatuations
Lily white fascinations of a
Black Love
Inevitably subjecting my heart to a
Dead end
Colorless pain

Childishly anticipating thinking
"Maybe he's the one"
When I know he full of shit
Yet, I continue to visualize him to be
My knight in shining armor hurrying to
Rescue me from
All the pain and suffering
I bring my own self to know and love
Galloping on his Black Stallion from
The Heavens above
Saving me from the evils of this world
Hey wake up girlfriend
Wake up from your dream world, when
In this reality that you refusing to see
This love you want to be
Will never be with he
Because he ain't shit
And you know this...shit

Why you keep attracting the same shit?
I keep attracting the same ole shit
Haven't cleared my sanity from the grime and grit
All the baggage that came wit

Yesterday's love lessons
Unlearned
That's why today I keep getting burned
Again

You know this shit is getting on my got damn nerves
Checking out astrological charts
Trying to keep myself on top of things
By being informed with
Top-secret planetary influences
Or the cosmic energies that could surface with
Our love connection
And even given that the Moon told me herself
His Sun was dried out
Lacking heat, making his feathers fly south
When my Venus love nature points northeast
I nevertheless continued to feast on
"But maybe he can, still be the one"
When I know he full of shit
Because he was yesterday
When I know our shit don't click
Because it didn't yesterday
And I have known him for years
So why have I subjected myself to this shit ...for years?

You know I'm starting to get on my own got damn nerves
Leveling my foot a few inches over the
Same pile of shit I stepped in
When I was sixteen years of age
Still engaged in childish tactics
Playing games with
Grown-ass kids
When what I'm starting to look like is
An idiot
Or how about a fool
For failing to use this rational tool above my shoulders called
A brain
It's profane that I still think this mud pie I've made
Is a Baskin Robbin's ice-cream cake

Now I'm really starting to get on my own
Got damn nerves so...
What am I going to do about it?

A Hard Day of Work

Hey Honey!
Go'on head and give me some money
I'll love ya real good if you just
Come to me
Shoooot...I'll get on my knees for another
Fifty?

Look I can't help how my mama raised me
And I'm out here hoe'n
Like I can't catch the HIV
Well trick'in ain't the same as prostitution to me
So enough of the comments
Just come and tap dis big booty
Cuz I sho'll need the money
To buy me a drink
Some smoke and
Sump'in to eat
For me and my child who's just as hungry
Plus I'm going club'in tonight
At the bar down the street
And I still gots to buy some hair and
Get my nails done by the Chinese

So come here baby!
Let me love you down
Don't be shy...just come to me

And you sho'll don't need to know
I got an STD!

WHAT DA HELL WRONG WIT YOU?

YOU KEEP DISRESPECTIN ME
WANNA RAISE YO VOICE
PUT YO HANDS ON ME

GET PLAY FROM YO BOYS
LIKE YOU REALLY DID SOMETHIN
WHEN YOU DISSED THAT YOUNG LADY
CALLED HER "SHADY"
CUZ SHE DIDN'T WANNA TALK TO YOU

NOW PERSONALLY
I WOULD HOPE THAT YOU COULD BEAT
A FEMALE'S ASS

BEING THAT YOUR PHYSIQUE
IS THAT OF A MATURE MAN
PERSONALITY THAT OF A FAG
AND SO WHAT YOU TRYIN TO
PROVE?
BY TREATIN ME WITH HATRED
REACHING ORGASM
EVERY TIME YOU DEGRADE ME

WHAT DA HELL WRONG WIT YOU?

YOU KEEP DISRESPECTIN ME
CUZ YOU CAN'T DEAL WITH THE
FACT THAT
I DON'T WANT TO HOLLA AT YOU!
SO NOW I'M A BITCH
CUZ YOU'ZA DRUNKEN FOOL
NOW GOT THE BALLS TO ACT UP
AND INVADE MY SPACE

WHEN LET'S FACE IT
YOU AND YOUR IGNORANT HOMIES
ARE THE ONES WHO BELONG TOGETHA
THE BUFFOONS WHO GET OFF ON
TORMENTING THEIR SISTAS

WHAT DA HELL WRONG WIT YOU?

DON'T YOU KNOW I'VE PEEPED YO GAME
A LITTLE DICK HAVIN BASTARD
AND I AINT SAYIN NO NAMES
WHILE YOU TOO SCARED TO STEP
TO THE DUDES IN YO HOOD
BUT IT'S ALL GOOD
BECAUSE YOU KNOW EXACTLY
WHAT YOU DO
WHICH GIVES ME THE LEGAL
RIGHT TO
REACH OUT AND CUT YOU

SO I'M JUST GONE SIT BACK
AND WATCH
YOUR EVERY MOVE
ACCUMULATE EVERY TIME YOU
DISRESPECT ME
THEN WHEN YOU LEAST EXPECT
ME TO
I'M GONE STAB YO PUNK ASS IN
THE KNEE...BOO

**WHAT THE HELL WRONG WIT
YOU?**

CAN WE BE FRIENDS?

HOW YOU GONE SAY
"WELL, CAN WE BE FRIENDS?"
LIKE I'M S'POSE TO CHECK YES ON A CONTRACT
WITH A BALL POINT PEN
YOU CAN'T DEVELOP A FRIENDSHIP
AS FAST AS YOU SIGN YO NAME
THAT LINE IS REAL TIRED
GET SOME NEW GAME

AM I SUPPOSE TO RESPOND WITH A GITTY, "OKAAY"
WHEN I'VE ONLY ASSOCIATED WITH YOU
IN LESS THAN A DAY
A FRIENDSHIP IS SOMETHING THAT IS
GROWN OVER TIME
WITH TRUST AND HONESTY
NOT WIT NO QUICK LINE
YOU CAN'T DEVELOP A FRIENDSHIP
AS FAST AS YOU SIGN YO NAME
THAT LINE IS REAL TIRED
GET SOME NEW GAME

HELL I'VE KNOWN PEOPLE FOR MANY YEARS
THOUGHT THEY WERE MY FRIENDS
BUT THEY LEFT ME IN TEARS
CAUSED BY MY MISTAKEN TRUSTWORTHINESS
SO YOU THINK I'M GONE FALL EASY FOR DAT
PLAYED-OUT MESS

DON'T USE THAT LINE WITH ME EVER AGAIN
I'D RATHER YOU BE BLUNT AND SAY
YOU WANNA SLIDE RIGHT IN AND
OUTTA OF MY FACE
YOU NEED TO RUN
WITH THAT TIRED OLE LINE
THAT'S BEEN BAKED, FRIED, AND
WELL DONE

SO QUIT RUSHIN
TRYIN TO BE SMOOTH
AND JUST TAKE YO TIME
AND SAVE THE LINES FOR THOSE FEMALES
WITH SENSE LESS THAN A DIME

YOU CAN'T DEVELOP A FRIENDSHIP
AS FAST AS YOU SIGN YO NAME
THAT LINE IS REAL TIRED
GET SOME NEW GAME

PLUS I ALREADY TOLD YA...I GOTTA MAN!

Gold Digger

You call me a "Gold Digger"
Because I desire beautiful things
Because I deserve beautiful things
Because I expect beautiful things
In order to obtain and maintain my love
Because I am a
Beautiful Thang!

You call me a "Gold Digger"
Because your Ego is so large and
Your pockets are so small
Making you quick to call a woman who
Simply enjoys receiving gifts
A "Captain Save-a-Hoe"
When it's really yo, lack of intellect and
Inability to
Distinguish between ladies who deserve gold and
Those who do not

Too ignorant to realize that
A woman who is good to you
Deserves to be treated as royalty
So if I am good to you
You need to start treating me
Like the Queen that I am
And give me all the gold I deserve!

Funk ───────────────────────────

Oh really
Is that Funk you feel?

Is that Funk you feel
When I put the **PERIOD** at the end of my statement.
The **EXCLAMATION POINT** at the end of my disagreement!
And the **QUESTION MARK** after I'm done checking you for playing
Spades?
When the suit is...
Diamonds
Those diamonds, you so busy trying to hold on to with the wrong
Queen!

Is that Funk you feel?
When my hands ABUSE the atmosphere
Or when my head moves from side to side, as I
Communicate this SENSITIVE subject matter?

Is that funk you feel?
When my tone INCREASES!
And my eyes send out a signal that says..."NIGGA WHAT!"

That might be Funk you feeling
That might be Funk you feeling
But I ask you...

Is that Funk you feel?
When my hands MOLEST your Gift
Or when my head lays on your left thigh
As I place a love bite on your right
In order to communicate these SENSUAL feelings I'm feeling?

Is that Funk you feel?
When my tone high, high...HEIGHTENS
And my eyes send out a signal that says, "BROTHER...
I'M GONE TEAR YOU UP!"

You see, that same Funk you heard when I said,
"Hell nawl...I ain't cooking dinner tonight!"

It's the same Funk you tasted two days ago when I made yo
ass
Bar-b-que chicken, greens, cornbread, macaroni & cheese, and...
Pecan Pie

That same Funk that burnt yo house down, right after
Ya bought brand-new furniture
It's the same Funk that kept you warm those many nights
You had a hard day at work

That Funk that flowed from my mouth and gave you
So-called "Attitude"
It's the same Funk that flowed from my lips and tongue
As I blessed your body with gratitude

That same Funk you see when my hips walk from side to side
In a "I don't give a F#! *K"!
Motion
It's the same Funk you feel when my hips rock
Forward and backwards in a
Riding-like motion

So before you place "Attitude" upon my person
Let us not forget
The PLEASURES that come with the PAINS
The GAINS with the GIVINGS
The LOVE with the HATE
The GRATITUDE with the "ATTITUDE"

Then and only then
Can you sit back and holistically enjoy
The Aromaaa of
My...Funk!

TIRED OF TAKING IN THE GROCERIES

I EXHALE FRUSTRATION AS I
PREPARE MYSELF FOR THIS COMPLEX TASK

ONE BAG ON MY RIGHT WRIST
ONE ON MY LEFT
TWO BAGS ON MY RIGHT ARM
TWO ON MY LEFT
THE GALLON OF WATER
GONE CHILL IN THE CAR FOR A FEW DAYS

ONE MIGHT SAY MY WAYS ARE LAZY
BUT I STAY ON THE 2ND FLOOR
CAN BARELY OPEN THE DOORS
AND I AIN'T MAKING TWO TRIPS!
THIS SHIT IS A TRIP
BECAUSE THE JOB IS FOR YOU
WHERE ARE YOU BOO?

I'M TIRED OF BEING A STRONG BLACK SINGLE SISTAH
COME GET WIT'HUH
AND TAKE IN THE DAMN GROCERIES!
CUZ I'M TIRED OF TAKIN' 'EM IN
ON MY OWN

Easier To Say Goodbye

Mistaken love
Forsaken trust
For the sake of my spirit
GOODBYE is a must

The insecurities and doubts that
Lingered around your heart
Suffocated to thoughtless, selfish actions

I had an eyelash
Defeated by gravity
Poking, causing an irritation
Causing a temporary blindness
Unable to see the lack of reflection
The differences in lifestyle
Ya see Honey, I gets high off life

Amused at love's insanity
She makes you laugh in pain
Drowned with a silliness
I thought I could change the direction your spirit was roaming

Thought you were mature enough to commit
Forgetting that you've been baking at a high temperature of
BOY, too long
Tough and dry
Thought I could simmer you into a tender tasteful MAN
Silly me, silly me

See, there was no need to caress me with lies
For I am a big girl and
I can take care of mine
So please continue not to worry about my feelings
They will be comforted by
The lesson
Learned

And this lesson I've learned in loving you
Brings me to
Send you on your way
Like the death of a dramatic day

Goodbye!

CANDY!

NEVER IGNORE
THAT BURSTING FLAVOR YOU GET
FROM THAT TINY PIECE OF CANDY

BECAUSE THE NEXT PIECE
YOU DECIDE TO POP IN YOUR MOUTH
WILL NOT SATISFY THAT HAUNTING HIGH
YOU GOT FROM THE FIRST

AND WE ALL KNOW
WHEN IT COMES TO EATING CANDY
THERE'S NO SUCH THING AS
A SECOND CHANCE!

FED UP

I'M TIRED OF LOOKIN AT YO FACE
SNEAKY EYES ALWAYS GRINNIN
SINNIN LIKE THE "HOE OF BABYLON"
PASSIN YO LOVE AROUND LIKE A
TRIATHLON
MISTAKIN' ME FOR A FOOL
WHEN YOU KNOW THAT I KNOW
I'VE GOTS MO' GAME THAN YOU

DON'T YOU KNOW THE TRUTH
WILL ALWAYS BE BROUGHT TO THE LIGHT
SO NO MATTER HOW TIGHT
YOU THINK YOUR PLAN MAY BE
WHEN THE PLOT OF CHEATIN ON ME
ENTERS YO DOME
MY FEMALE INTUITION WILL LEAD ME STRAIGHT HOME
AND CATCH YOU SLIPPIN

NOW YA TRIPPIN CUZ I'M FED UP AND
IT AIN'T NOTHIN YOU CAN DO ABOUT IT
SO I'M SWEEPIN' YOU TO THE SIDE LIKE A BROOM
AND YOU BETS WATCH YO BACK CUZ
I'M SENDING YO ASS TO THE
"UPPAH ROOOOOM"

Pacifier

Wanna be a baby?
Want mama to take care of you?
Wanna be a child?

Want mama to nag about completing your life chores?
Wanna be a boy?
Want mama to remind you of such?

Wanna get yo chill on?
Ignore the future
Ignore the present
Savor the past
Savor ignorance
Wanna be a boy?

Hey man!
Wanna be a boy?

Well come suck on my nipple
I know you can do that well

Come suck on my nipple like you suck on dem blunts
Like you suck on dat 40-ounce
Like you suck on dem cats
Dem alley cats
And in some cases
Dem tomcats

Come boy
Suck on my nipple
Since your limbs have stopped there
Boy

Come suck on my nipple
Like you suck on dem automobiles
Like you suck on dat basketball
Like you suck on dem gats

Come boy

Please suck on my nipple
And become a Man!

Come suck on my nipple
And let me give you life
Let me nourish you with the reality of a Man
The reality I've been missing

Come boy suck on my nipple
And let me nourish you with my Womanliness
My Motherliness
My Queenliness
And taste my milk
Taste a Woman
Then become a Man!

Taste my strength
Taste my weakness
Taste my sensitivity
Taste my insecurities
Taste my forehead and my backside!

Come suck on my nipple and become full of life
Become full with my life
And learn me
Learn how to please me

Become my reflection
Reflect my strength
Come boy
Suck on my nipple
And become
My King!

Red Zone

Forgot to count the days but
I know it's vastly approach'n
'Cause my back ache'n
Stomach bloat'n
And so I'm over here hope'n
You'd get outta my face expeditiously
Because it's starting to make me
A little irritated
And 'roun dis time
I'm not gone let you get away with
Anything!

So if you wanna bring yourself around me
During these five to seven days
Watch me hell raise for seems like no reason
Well please then, make yourself comfortable and at
home
But you better buckle up and sit tight
You're now entering
The Red Zone!

So our tones commence to rising
Disturbing the waters
Placing more heartache on our relations
Because you still not facing this reality
Nor trying to understand
I'm a Woman
And I'm going through the motions
While Motrin over-the-counter
Ain't doing a damn thang!

My neck
My back
My neck and my back

I just wanna smack the shit outta sump'n,
Just because
You see it's hard for me to feel any love
Because all I feel is these damn cramps
Popping pills
Mad at Eve for bite'n dat apple
Feeling spiteful that I have to suffer
And he don't
And so I won't give him any peace
Except for a piece of my mind

Every month one of my children dies
Shedding away their life
Then you wonder why
I'm so emotional and dramatic
Creating static
Don't want to be bothered
Just wanna mourn on my own
Let me be me
I'm in the Red Zone!

So as my moods now swing
Drama-filled conversations start to bring
Chaotic thoughts of
"What the fuck is goin'zone!"
I'll let you know now
You have entered...
The Red Zone!

Gray Hairs on My Pussy

I've got gray hairs on my pussy
And I ain't talkin 'bout no pet kitty cat
I'm talkin 'bout the one that lies dead smack
'Tween my thighs
And I know that she's wise and knowledgeable and thangs but
She's too young and too vibrant to be going gray
Which conveys to me that
You must be causing girlfriend stress!

She must be worried and concerned that
You're trying to insert her with
Drama
When all dis lil mama wants is
Some good lovin
Some affection
Consideration
A couple smooches here and there would be nice
Some honesty
Loyalty
Monogamy would be just fine
Which would probably take her mind off

Why you didn't come home the other night and
Why it took you so long to get one?
And I bet it's this type of unnecessary bullshit!
That she's turning gray from

To Please You

Can you blame me for giving up my love so quickly?
Look at the color of your back
Your thighs
I just want to embrace your body with my
Heaven-sent lips
I just want your presence
Your security
Your protection

I just want to please you,
Thus pleasing me

So let me give you something to indulge and digest
Quenching your insatiable thirst
Thus quenching mine
Fulfilling your innermost desires
Thus fulfilling mine

I just want to please you,
Thus pleasing me

So don't place judgment
Mislabeling my actions as
Promiscuity
Because I choose to give you me, now
Because I choose to let your eyes adore every inch of me, now
And your hands caress every part of me, now
While your manhood fills the core of me, now
Because I simply desire
That your desires for me
Be experienced, now

I just want to please you,
Thus pleasing me

So open and receive
These gifts I am eager to give
Ending my suffering of wanting you
Needing you

Longing for you to till my garden
So that I can bear fruit
Providing nourishment to keep you growing
To keep us growing

I just want to feed you,
Nourish you,
Thus nourishing me

Why not today?
Why not now?
Why must I wait?
Why can't you show?
Why can't you see?
Why must you. . . .

Why must you ignore and
Run away from
All that is good
All that I am
All that I have to give
And I'll give all that I can

To please you
Thus pleasing me

An Attempt

Every word that spills from his lips
Entraps me
A speech so rare and divine
Where his mind fathoms perfect images of
Beauty and Love
That his mouth opens and projects through
Motion pictures of romance
A hint of drama and a
Touch of comedy
Desiring peace and harmony
Yet his actions are quite contradictory
Making way for a murder mystery
Which is a totally different story altogether
An entirely new poem

So getting back and attempting to stay on track
I adore his warm snuggles and his
Tender hug
Those dreamy eyes and
Boyish charm
And though I know he means me no harm
His verbals still produce harmful effects that
His lack of action causes
Don't he know that all he has in this world is
His balls and his word
I'm starting to get a little perturbed
Which is a totally different story altogether
An entirely new poem

So getting back and attempting to stay on track
He has great form
A pleasant stroke
And a mean backhand
Making a woman feel like everything
Then as his pendulum swings
She feels like nothing at all
But as I keep trying to tell yawl!
That's a whole new story altogether
An entirely new poem

This poem right here, right now
Was inspired by the romantic feelings
His language brings
But I'm having a difficult time bringing myself to
Stay entrapped in his
Played-out words

Fuck what ya heard, it's all about what you do!
I've had enough of the talking from you
So if you want my lovin, you now gots to pursue me with
Actions
Because it's apparent that your words are lacking
Bond
I don't know who told you, you were the "Don"
But sorry sweetie...you're not!
So please pack up your acting suit
You'll receive no Academy Award here
And thank you for such a wonderful performance
I appreciate the humor...my dear!

I Love Me Some Him

A just right size
Hard and at attention
Ready to please me and
Not to mention that
My mouth salivates at
The thought of him

Strong
Stiff
Long-standing
Committed with loyalty
He is righteous
He is royalty
And so I treat him oh so royal
He makes my heart flutter
He makes my waters boil
As his
Chocolate, caramel, vanilla
Toils rhythmically between my
Awaiting hips
While my lips hug him hungrily
And he fills my belly
With pleasure
Nothing can measure
The satisfaction he gives
And I

Love
Me
Some
Him

Can A Sistah Get Some...?

Can a sistah get some...
Righteous love'n ... consecutively?
Why is it that you gotta go and act...ig'nantly?
Then I'm forced to pop my
Nipple out yo mouth, then
Subject my delicate ears to your
Cry'n and hollerin'
Just to get you to recognize that
You can't take a sistah's love for granted
You just can't take a woman's generosity for granted

Now granted I enjoy your skillful dick and
The pleasant stroke it gives
But this sistah ain't about to live with nor accept any
Bullshit
I'm not about to give my mind or my time to
A Negro who's not aware of, nor acknowledges
My worth
And it hurts me as much as it hurts you
To use my precious puh'nah'ny as a
Disciplinary tool
But I refuse to let your "negative energy"
Enter into my sacred

And so now I gots to suffer with
An innate need, not being fed
Placing pillows between my legs
'Cause you wanna start act'n elementary
When alls a sistah want is...some righteous love'n
Consecutively!

Now it's not that I enjoy these yearly gaps or
Monthly holdbacks
That I don't necessarily have to experience, if I choose
For a dick does come a dime a dozen
It's just that I prefer some conscious love'n
'Cause I ain't into all that fuss'n and fight'n
Force'n a man to treat me like a Queen
I'm not interested in exhausting my power
In a hopeless attempt to persuade or manipulate brotha
To handle me a certain way
If Mr. Man don't gracefully choose to, then
He can be on his way
For I know something greater
Will inevitably, be delivered to me

Though a sistah rather receive some...righteous love'n
Consecutively

Forehead & Backside

Round and protruding
Combined they are exuding
Electricity

A chemistry that is
Cosmic

And when felt together...
Boy oh boy do they come with an
Authority!

Never seen or heard before
They roar!
And if you re not ready for their
Truth
You bets run and hide

Taste the collective forces of My... Forehead and Backside!

MS. ATTITUDE

I KNOW I USE UP A LOT OF ENERGY
BEING EVIL EVERY DAY
CONSTANTLY REMINDING MYSELF
NOT TO LOOK YO WAY

    OR IF I DECIDE TO
    I GOTS TO GIVE YOU A NASTY STARE
    CUZ YOU LOOK LIKE THE TYPE
    MY MAN MIGHT LIKE
    AND I MUST KEEP YOU AWARE OF THIS FACT!
    I AM JUST AS FINE
    AND THIS MAN STANDING BESIDE ME
    WILL FOREVER BE MINE

YOU JUST THINK YOU ALL THAT
CUZ YO HAIR DONE ALL UP AND
YO BODY IS NICE
WHEN I BET YOU A SLUT
I SEE PAST THE HYPE
THINKING YOU SO FINE
I CAN TELL BY YO WALK
SWAYING DEM HIPS SIDE TO SIDE

    YO LIFE LOOK SO HAPPY
    WHEN MINE IS SO TIE'D!

        WHY SHE LOOKING AT ME LIKE THAT?
        SHE DON'T KNOW ME AT ALL
        I CAN'T HELP THE FACT THAT I WALK
        WITH MY HEAD UP AND STANDING TALL
        I COULD BE YOUR COUSIN
        OR EVEN SISTA!
        THAT YOU NEVER KNEW
        AND YOU WALKING AROUND HERE ACTING
        LIKE I'VE DONE SOMETHING TO YOU!

        I LOVE GOD AND MYSELF SO MUCH
        MY PEOPLE I COULD NEVER HATE
        I CAN'T BURN ANY BRIDGES

CUZ I KNOW NOT MY FATE
OR WHERE IT MAY END UP
I MIGHT HAVE TO WORK WITH YOU
SO STOP LOOKING AND ACTING
LIKE I'VE DONE SOMETHING TO YOU!

WHY CAN'T YOU SMILE BACK AT ME?
WE'VE BEEN THROUGH THE SAME THANGS
MY FAMILY TOO HAS BEEN DEFAMED AND
TIED UP IN CHAINS
SO WORK WIT ME SISTA
LET'S EASE OUR PEOPLE'S PAIN
CUZ I'M SICK AND TIRED OF HAVING TO
MAKE MY FACE LOOK "HARD"
AND EVERY TIME I SEE YOU
I GOTS TO PUT UP MY GUARD

SO GIVE IT UP SISTA
IT'S TIRED
AND IT'S MAKING YO FACE UGLY!
I WON'T HAVE TO TAKE YO MAN
BECAUSE HE GONE GLADLY RUN TO ME
WE GONE NEED EACH OTHER ONE DAY
AND THOUGH YOU DENY THIS
IT IS SO VERY TRUE
SO STOP LOOKING AND ACTING
LIKE I'VE DONE SOMETHING TO YOU

MS. ATTITUDE
WHY YA SO RUDE TO ME?
WHEN I'M YOUR SISTA AND
YOU MIGHT NEED ME SOMEDAY

Discontinue the Dis'n the Brotha Sessions

You walk around displaying your
Butt, Breast, and Thighs
Then wonder why
I just wanna slide
Right in!
Then you go have that "Doggin Out Session"
Wit yo girlfriends
Talkin 'bout the Black Man

It's in our nature
Not because we hate-cha
So if you willing to give it up
You bets believe
We gone take ya

Now I must admit
That you have the ultimate decision
Whether we'll have sex or not
But you so busy competing, scratching, and growling
Wit yo own sista
I gets a lot
Of yo lovin!

So before you decide to
Participate in those
"Dis'n the Brotha Sessions"
Try to realistically look within yo'self
Cuz you da one give'n up yo goodies!
Like Santa's little Hoes...I mean
Elves!

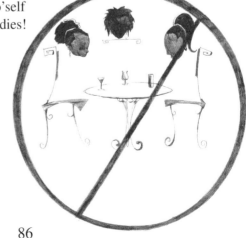

I Don't Need To...

One might say that I've got a long way to go
Before I'll ever know
How to acquire and satisfy a Good Man
Due to the low number of years
My physical body has been on this Earth
They over look the centuries
My soul has been floating over this terrain

You see I don't need to experience
Several bad relationships
Before I know what it takes to, Acquire
A GOOD Man

To acquire a GOOD Man
You must be a GOOD Woman
It's called your reflection

See if my actions are stank
I'm gone look stank
I'm gone smell stank
And a GOOD Man don't want
A stank'in woman

Now stank is when you are wearing an outfit
That looks like underwear
Stank is when yo attitude is the size of yo big azz
Hanging out yo outfit
That looks like underwear
Point being, if you stank...
Men gone treat you like their underwear
Which means even though ya stank
And he knows ya stank
Because he done picked you up and sniffed you
He still gone wear you, out
Until the elastic is loose
Fabric is worn and
Holes are all over the place
And when he's finally tired of
Smell'in and look'in at yo stank'in azz

87

He gone toss you to the side like
Dirty laundry

Now when you act and dress appropriately
Only then can a GOOD Man notice your true beauty
Instead of focusing on your Big Booty

Only when you're a Good Woman
Only then you'll attract a Good Man
Only when you're a Good Woman
Only then you won't accept less than a Good Man
It's called your reflection

You see I don't need to experience
Several bad relationships
Before I know what it takes to, Satisfy
A GOOD Man

To satisfy a Good Man,
You have to be understanding
Which means you can't be so
"Demanding"

I'm a woman; I want attention and affection all the time
He's a man; he just wants to watch Sports Center
I'm a woman; I just want good communication
He's a man; he's fine with a good ejaculation
Then yawl can talk about Sports Center

He's a man; he has an Ego
He's a man; he doesn't feel like talking today
He's a man; he wants to hold the remote
He's a man; he's going to lie
He's a man; you're going to catch him in a lie
He's a man and
He's just different!
Now ladies, don't get me confused

I ain't one of those weak passive women
Who's been mentally abused
I've just recognized the mistakes I've made
And I've learned that if you repeat the same a
That have caused you stress
You will continue to walk along that same path o
Stank azz relationships!

So as you see, I don't need to experience
Several bad relationships
Before I know what it takes to acquire a Good Man
I don't need to experience
Several bad relationships
Before I know what it takes to satisfy a GOOD Man

Because I have come to understand
The power lies in my hands

Returning The Favor

How dare you continue to sleep with my man
When you know he suppose to be in a
Committed relationship
Along with your awareness of whom it's with
Then in the same breath
You wanna voice that Black Men ain't worth
A sip of cheap wine
Well if you cultivate yo own and
Stop mess'n with mine
Then I'm sure they wouldn't behave
In the way that they do

Now I know that my commitment is with him
So it would be of no significance
If I were to check you
You can't help being
The conniving woman that you are
Too lazy to work on molding ya own

Yet nevertheless,
We must respect each other as
Women, Wives, and Mothers
If we want him to respect and
Treat us like Queens
Now maybe my morals are too high
For you to follow
But if your man approaches me
In an intimate way
And informs me he has a lady
I ain't gone be shady
I will send him back home to you
The same way he came
Pants zipped and goods unused
At least by me

You see I'm not the one to share a penis
This here Highness too greedy for that
I like my man's pleasure smelling fresh and
Looking clean
Kept far away from the
Starving dick fiends

So if one day mine looks real tempting
And you just wanna try some
Put yourself in my shoes and
Think how you'd feel
If you was the one being downright disrespected

So the only thing I ask of you
Is to do unto others as you want done to you
Simply called
Returning the favor

I Hate The Playa and I Hate The Game

Thought I was the shit
Not purposely intimidating those brothers who
Seek to stroll down my path
It's only my expertise of being an unnatural single woman
That has my horns roaring
But his games got my horns roaring
Pouring a taste of my own medicine down my throat

Are you interested or just playing a game?
Is it a shyness or is it a game that you play?
Your subtle flirtations lead my mind astray
Your eye seductions make my emotions sway
Are you feeling me?
Or is it a game you play?

Like a little girl who has a crush on her
Older brother's best friend
I'm so nervous when
His energies are felt
I melt when his intense eyes are seen
And I find that in my solitude
I constantly dream about
Making love to him
But the games he play, makes our future dim
Have me not knowing what to think
Or what to do
So I'm now afraid to
Express my feelings
So I don't express my feelings
Yet I know he gots to sense these feelings
Which heavily pulsate through my veins
But this Playa still choose to
Play the game

Mr. Church Man ———————————————

Come by my house
Let us cipher on the Universe and
Its laws
Come to my church!

Though it won't serve any swine
It will entice and move yo mind
Satisfy yo hunger
Which is a whole lot juicier
Than those ribs and dat roni you desire
I can ignite your fire

And no, I'm not religious
However, highly spiritual
Which means it's not purely physical or
For show
I don't need a bad suit to go
It's mentally embedded in my dome, like stone
So go on head if you want to
Look for your bride to be at
The United Church of the only sanctified
For you will surely miss out on a good loyal woman

Too shallow to feel my Godly soul
Too blind to see my strength
Too dumb to know a Good Black Woman
When she's standing right by yo side
Just because she don't sit by yo side
In their church

Ok, you refrain from those "sinful" pleasures
Well so do I and
So can the next man
But tell me, Mr. Church Man,
How can you stand distinct
From those at yo church
Whose loving spirit is extinct and
Cast me to Hell

Point their finger at me
Since I don't cry out to their defined "Trinity"
I still kneel and pray every day to one God
Our God
Are we not living the same order?
Are we not seeking the same goals?
I want to satisfy the Almighty
I want to please Him as you
So why is my good intent ignored?
Why is my inner beauty abhorred?
When I live for the Lord as well

Hey Mr. Church Man!
Open up dat mind and exit that shell
Look away from dat idol for just one second
And maybe...just maybe
You'll get that supreme joy you've been praying for
For all these years

Intimidation

Intimidation
Something all strong sisters must deal with

Excuse us for having knowledge of self
Excuse us for recognizing what we deserve
And not expecting less

Excuse us for not wanting to be like "Mike"
For not putting up with "Ike"
Excuse us for our abundance of strength

Intimidation is felt only by the weak
Only the weak ...
Let intimidation restrain them from pursuing
Something all strong sisters must deal with

Excuse me for slapping you in the face
When you pinched me on my ass
Excuse me for telling you how it is
After you ignorantly requested my lovin

Excuse me for telling you to
Go to HELL and
Get outta my house
When you entered my domain as a drunken fool
Excuse me for hanging up on you
When you cursed at me
Like you didn't know whom you were talking to

Intimidation is felt only by the weak
Only the weak...
Let intimidation restrain them from pursuing
Something all strong sisters must deal with!

Sometimes

Sometimes
Sometimes when I look in your eyes
I see honesty
I see sensuality

But you know sometimes
When I look in your eyes
I see lies
I see bullshit

Sometimes
Sometimes when I kiss your lips
I taste
Ooooh, I taste satisfaction
I taste a sweet sweet nectar

But you know sometimes
When I kiss your lips
I taste displeasure
A sour bitterness

Sometimes
Sometimes when you rub my back
I feel security
I feel a strong confidence

But you know sometimes
When you rub my back
I feel insecurities
A sense of doubt

You know sometimes
Sometimes when we make love to each other
I sense a growing warmth
A deep yearning

But sometimes when we make love to each other
I sense a cold indifference
A dying lust

Sometimes
Sometimes I feel love
But you know sometimes
I feel hate
But I guess this comes with loving you
Love is a funny thing isn't it?
Love is a funny thing

Say My Name

You insensitively call me a "Trick"
Got the nerves to call me Yo "Hoe"
Don't you know you were shaped in my womb?
Which would make you the same thang, bro'

You have the audacity to call me a "Bitch"
When my split
Dilated ten centimeters to give you life
Quit being so got damn trife!
And stop disrespecting
Ya Mama
Stop disrespecting me because
I am...
Yo MAMA!

I am your SISTER
Your LOVER
Your DAUGHTER
Slaughter those conditioned thoughts and
Ill notions
The slave master implanted within your mind
360 degrees ago
Because you'll reap what you sow
Taste the Karma of your actions
Get what you give
And when Yo kids begin treating you the same
Don't be preaching
"These young'uns nowadays be acting a shame"

So say my name, say my name
QUEEN MOTHER EARTH!
Cleanse the dirt and filth from Yo mouth
Singing to me a
Sweet melodic song
As you journey righteously along
Back to your natural state
Returning home
Let's create the Queen' dome
Placing me upon my throne
As you acknowledge my name
Revere my name
Say my name and
Save your soul

Be Careful What You Wish For

I asked for my reflection
Prayed for him to be sent

Unaware of my lack of awareness
Though comfortable with Self
At least the portion I want to accept
Running from the other
In hopes that it never reveals

I asked for my reflection
Prayed for him to be sent
Unaware of the total person being revealed
Now placed in black and white
And I so easily want to turn away and say
Would ya come back later?
I need to work this one out on my own
Yet the clock has already struck twelve
And my total person has been revealed

I can no longer hide the warts
Nor the beauty
It already swims through my mind
Like a goldfish in a drinking glass

I asked for my reflection
Prayed for him to be sent
And the Negro is just like me!

Be careful what you ask for
Cuz you just might get it

Sistahs

We
Fed from the same placenta
Nourished along the same cord that brought us
Fruits and wines
We loved each other

We loved each other before he loved us
We knew each other

We knew each other before we knew each other
For we shared the same space and time
As our vehicles formed in darkness
Blackness
Purity

Together we flew in the known and
Swam in the unknown
As we prepared ourselves for the pains of perfection
We comforted each other for we knew
The cold, shivering, draining dis-ease
That would soon surround us
Could consume us
Consuming our thoughts, creating an unreality
We'd defend wholeheartedly to be the supreme
And this would go on for what would seem like
Eternity
If either one of us fell weak

If either one of us fell weak, this dis-ease
This virus
Would send hypnotic vibrations throughout our Universal bodies
Producing a smothering illusion that we were strangers
That we were not of the same and
Our duties differed
A prevailing illusion that would bring us
Mental heartache
Physical pain
So we held tight

We held tight as graceful contractions
Delivered us into
Evolution
We held tight and we prayed that we would never weaken
Never crack
Remaining immune to the virus
That desperately hungered to feed off our souls
We held tight and
We Sistahs
Were born

Born into this physical realm
With the same blood running through our veins
Nursing on the same breast
Resting heads on the same chest
Same kinda cat sitting 'tween our thighs
Same roles
Same responsibilities
Same abilities
We
Sistahs
Born

As we progressed throughout our early years
We grew near and near
Then stopped
Fell asleep a minute too long
Misguided
Mis-educated
Misinterpreted
Misunderstood
Misery loves company
And the company us Misses kept
Kept us weak
Weakened our immunity
And we let
The virus
In

It split us into halves
Then quarters
Then eighths
Which made us look like them
To...them chickens
To those
To...those hoes
To dat
To...dat BITCH, "I'll fuck her man anyway"

Same kinda cat sitting 'tween our thighs
Same roles
Same responsibilities
Same abilities
However contracted the misconceived inability
To see reality for what it was, is, and will always be
We Sistahs
Forgot we are Sistahs
And we became that same virus
Hungrily feeding on each other's pains, weaknesses
We became that same virus
Thirsting to see how we can keep each other down
Starving to hear of the dis-ease she's falling victim too so
I fucked your man
Then you fucked hers

I found humor in your tears
And you brought her disrespect
To keep hers pouring

I found pleasure in your pain
So you turned your pain into Hell
For every man who slept within your thighs or even tried
To understand you
Diminishing the possibilities of becoming a man
For every male child that came from your womb

I contributed to your mis-education

And so you mis-educated every female formed in your sacred
Or raised in your home
And they became my daughter's daughters' worst enemies
And my son's strongest crutch

You know...them chickens
Those Hoes
Dat Bitch
You know... they
My...very own Sistah

Same Mother
Same Father
Same Grace

Same blood running through our veins
Same kinda cat sitting 'tween our thighs
Same roles
Same responsibilities
Same abilities
My Sistah
My only Sistah
With all sincerity
I apologize
Please forgive me
For we need we
Our union completes the prophecy
Puttin these jokers in their proper place
Let's embrace and fly together again
Hold tight our hands
Healing this injured land
With an unrelenting force
Never to weaken
Never to crack
Never to forget that we are Sistahs

For We
Are
Sistahs!

Family Reunion

Cornbread
Black-eyed peas
Candy-coated yams and a
Bar-b-que neck bone
Too tired, too full to go home
Feet resting upon a chair
Relaxing my head
Jelly jar in hand
Filled with my favorite flavor Kool-Aid
RED!

Y'all better get some peach cobbler up in here
Cuz y'all know me
Know what I'm about
Know what I likes
Red light, green light...that's my car
You see I'm trying to take y'all way back far
When mama said, "Don't make me..."
When mama said, "Don't make me.........Get Up!"
So I strut myself the other way
Far away from dat switch
Cuz we all know, mama fixin to trip

Tell yo mama I said give me a call
The last time I seen you
You was 'bout this tall!

Union
Coming together
Whenever
There's Ups & Downs
To the birth of a new seed
To the transcending of a soul
To infinity
We....Union
We come together
Whenever
There's Ups & Downs
Love it when you frown
Love it when you smile

Love you for you
Cuz you are
Family
A Commonality

Don't you know yo Auntie's cousin's niece's daughter
Pauline
She got eyes just like my sister's second daughter
Barbara Jean

Commonality
Because we Family
And we loves to Union
Our Family Reunion
Alive and well!
Can't you tell
It's so good to see you
God bless you as we union
As we enjoy our
Family Reunion

Yeah, Uncle Tyrone still actin a fool
Shawn Shawn just had another baby
And the daddy still crazy
Cousin Henry still sick
But no matter the hard times
We gone stick together
Forever
Cuz we are Family
And tomorrow, today
This very second is not promised to you

Yeah sometimes Mama ain't cool
Unc can act a damn fool
And my Cuz may be on drugs
And so sometimes
I just don't want 'em around me
But my heart forever holds love
Because you are
My Family

And we need each other
My sisters, my brothers, my family
Let's unite
Let's union at this Reunion
Appreciate the Commonality
Appreciate our Family
And let's stay together
Whenever
There's Ups & Downs

My United Family

Let's Wake Up

As you ponder and make love to your confusion
To your limits and boundaries
As you fuck your conditioned thoughts and
Molest your ego
I continue to be impregnated with ignorance
Doubt
Fear

Birthing insignificant questions
Receiving illogical answers
As I overindulge in your meaningless
Make-believe actions
Hearing shit that wasn't said
Seeing shit that didn't happen

And so I now begin making love to your
Confusion
I know begin fucking your
Conditioned thoughts
Your limits and boundaries
That I have now, made my own

Vice versa
We begin to fuck each other's confusion
Limits and boundaries
Simultaneously thinking we're making love
We're in love
We're establishing a relationship
We're "boyfriend and girlfriend"
"Husband and wife"
And it's soooo good!
It was...sooo good
It can be so good...again!
Maybe?
Maybe not

You know we've been together for seven years
But we have not been together
I've lived with him for fifteen years but
I've never lived with him

Married to him for thirty-five years but
We have never been married a day

Girl my man, he just be
He just be, work'in me
Ooooh daddy, you know the way I like it
As I reach, reach...
Orgasm
Thinking I'm about to get one
Thinking I've gotten one
But I haven't gotten a damn thang!
I've gotten an illusion of a feeling that got me believing
I'm gettin good lov'in
Because I'm gettin all the touch'in and hugg'in
When really I ain't gett'in shit
Because we ain't do'in shit!

We ain't talk'in 'bout shit
We ain't think'in shit
We ain't build'in shit
So we ain't becom'in...shit

I've known him since my kindergarten years
Reunited we believe
But I am he and he is I and
I know him and he knows me but
We're dreaming thinking that we don't
Thinking we're trying to get to know each other better
Thinking it's brand new but
He's dreaming and I'm dreaming
All the while wondering
When we gone wake the fuck up and see
Ain't nothing new under the sun!
There is no separation
I'm not looking at him and he not I
We're looking at ONE
One image
The same image
We're looking at GOD

So as soon as closed minds open and
Heavy eyes widen and
Plugged ears unplug and
Locked jaws become unlocked
Divine Love can be experienced
Living as ONE

Let's wake up and become ONE
Experience ONE
Not making love to each other but
Masturbating with self
Bringing self from this dream sleep
Let's wake up and be
ONE

I Wonder

As I gaze upon my body's bliss
Of winding curves and
Rounding hips
That rhythmically sway
Inside valley ways
Toward mountain tops, way high

Soft thighs that disperse sweet fragrant smells
From a flowering field
That fills the air
With a colorful love so true
So how can you even fix your lips and
Ask me for some "ass"!

Just wondering how long you'll be blind to my beauty

Hearing my deep sensual voice
As we talk on the phone exchanging game
While late night pouring rains
Rain sensual sounds
That subtly background
My untamed tongue
That righteously spits
Full of intellect and wit
So don't have my voice straining
With unnecessary rhetoric
From your instigated arguments of
Sharp cutting words and
Unheard feelings

Just wondering how long you'll be deaf to my music

Sitting back
Relaxing
Thinking about my many methods of pleasure
From cooking to baking
Sucking to tasting
Backwardly bending to
Accommodate your feelings
Or should I say...large Ego

Then here you go an
Ungraciously act
As if my pleasures were a commodity
For the nerve of he
To come with such stupidity

Just wondering how long you'll be ignorant of my worth
Just wonder how long you'll be,
Blind, deaf, and ignorant to who and what I am?

I wonder?

Your Ego Makes We Go

Did someone tell you it was cute?
Is this the reason you're behaving as if it were?
Well if they did, I'm here to tell you that
They surely lied!

See, I have tried on many occasions to ignore it
Acting as if it, isn't creating any problems
Disregarding
Its drama
And so it grows larger and larger
Moving us farther and farther apart

Can't you see that your prideful attempts to
"Save face"
Only complicate our relationship
Making it more difficult to connect
Opening doors for disrespect to enter
Can't you see that keeping your masculine macho'ism
Front and center
Only hinders YOUR growth
It only hinders YOUR progression
It keeps you from learning YOUR lessons
Constantly blocking YOUR blessings
Not mine

So you can to keep your mind
Closed shut
If you wish
But let me tell you this...
It's not a striking characteristic
Especially when you start acting like it's
Something to be proud of
When what it really does is
Create an appearance of ignorance
A "no reason to be"
Stubborn fool
Sweetie, it ain't cool or cute
You should really think about being mute sometimes and
Really listen for a change
You might learn something or two

That will benefit Self

But oh no, I keep forgetting
You don't need any help because
You know every mutha'fuckin thang and
You're never wrong
Failing to see how your actions bring about those
Sad songs called
The "Blues"
"My baby done left me," is what I'm fixin to do
For it's too much stress
And it is not hard to guess that

It's your Ego
Making we go through
Drama fo
No productive reason

So I refuse to keep feed'n it
Because it stinks...P U
And I really think, I'm not the only one who
Feels this way
Your folks probably don't tell you because
They're afraid that you may, cut up
But me, I don't give a fuck
I'm gone tell you regardless
And just hope that you don't take this negatively
Because it's all in love

Excuse me Mr. Man...you can shove your
Big Fat Azz Ego
Down someone else's throat
Because I can't take it no mo
I'm trying to open up and grow, yet

Your very large Ego
Keep try'n to make me go through
Drama fo
No constructive reason...at all!

He Get It From His Mama

Pointing flexing fingers
Mutate into stiff chrome-plated 45's
Blasting, shooting, buck, buck, buckin'
While both parties duckin' from the blame and
Who's responsible?
So I take the responsibility, I take the blame from
The weaker element

Not saying that it's weaker to cause detriment
However, saying it to acknowledge truth
All human life comes through
Me and mine
Meaning his mind
Is greatly influenced by the words that
I profess
Actions that I manifest
So I no longer protest and debate on
Who's at fault for
The chaos between your
Black Woman, Black Man, Black Family
I no longer reprimand him for the drama
Because in all honesty
"He gets it from his mama"
And it gets more severe with the lack of

So when these so- called "Thugs"
"Hip-Hop and R&B brahs"
Want to enviously flex their illusionary
Big bankroll
Via the quantity of hoes who
Prance around half-naked in their videos to
Entice someone to pay dem mind cuz
Their lyrics sho'll do...not
I take it as a compliment

Because I know without the scent
Or imagery of my puh'nah'ny
Money can't get made
Bricks won't get laid
Rent failed to be paid

114

Blunts never blazed
Doughnuts not glazed
And the entire economy is now searching for ways
To get us out of this unexpected deficit
All because I ceased the profiting of
My pussy
And "I know gay...you're not gay...he's gay!....
My brother's gay!"
But nevertheless, "No one can turn down this pussy!"
"Puss, puss, puuuhhsssy"

Please excuse me for being so frank
But it is where the power lies
Grows and strengthens
And I may get pastors and deacons who will
Ferociously retort
Stating proverbs from scriptures written by men
Describing the ghy'na to be a haven of sin
And so I sinfully say to they
"Fuck what you heard or what you read"
All life comes from between my legs
And so my friends
He can only get it from me, his mama
And it gets more severe with the lack of

So if your mind is still baffled at why he does not
Know the meaning of hard work
Or why it hurts him to pay a sistah her proper respect
Check into his foundation
Paying close attention in his
Relationship with
Him mama

Baby boys never properly nurtured by mama
Never given the opportunity to suckle on her breast
Left to be sculpted by egotistical air-filled chests of
Neighborhood Negroes
Then you wonder why he goes and says some shit like
"Fuck these bitches...ain't nuttin but hoes and tricks...
Lick on deez nuts and..."

What type of madness is this?
And how does it perpetuate?

From Queens who continue to make the mistake
And ungratefully take
Our gift to create
Then use it for their own selfish reasons
Why failing to see them as the cause of their pain
Ignition to the flames
That constantly defame
The African American Family

Thus it is necessary
That the woman lives more
Consciously
Because most likely He
Get it from his mama
And it's more severe with the lack of

Unveiling Eve

As I stand here and relax I
Breathe
Inhaling and
Exhaling

Inhaling thy grace bestowed upon me
When thee
Created we, in her image
I exhaaaale, deception
Falsification and defamation
Subjected towards our spirits
Where it has acquainted my people with a state of dis-ease
I breathe

Truth, Order, and Harmony
Regurgitate the fact that we
Fail to believe
Our minds have been conditioned for centuries
Processed
Like a No-Lye Hawaiian Silky
Thinking we are something that we are not
Forgetting that we got what we got
As soon as she formed
The Twat

Granting us magick to create
Conferring nurture with our embrace
For her, he has come through
And through her only, can mind states be made anew

Ripping through civilizations destroying statues
Banishing all signs and symbols of our rule
Using religion as a tool to
Perpetuate his lie
Why don't we look at their history?
Uncover the mystery
Simultaneously keeping in mind that we
Have been bamboozled
Our behaviors are learned

From Aryan invaders who burned towns
Families killed
Wives taken as prisoners
Ancient Egyptian teachings they cultured
Withered
As they struggled for white male dominance
Telling tales flipping scripts
Making it unnaturally switch
From Matriarchal to Patriarchal
Being watchful of every law passed and every story told
Persuasively showed in nearly every Biblical book
They shook the masses with the
Paradise myth

Revering Eve to the exile of all humankind
From the Garden of Bliss
Portraying her as a God-defying sexually seductive temptress
Thereby justifying all women to be regarded as mindless
When they're the ones blinded from the
Biological truth of birth
For man could have not been made first
Simple childhood fable fairytales telling fibs
Some bullshit bout woman being formed from
Man's ribs
When the Laws of Nature bring us to know that the
Female does not come from male
But the male through the female
His tales, his stories, are a plotted game
Man takes the credit while the woman endures the pain
And it's a damn shame

It's a shame their own women had to fight for their rights
While we fought for ours
Like wilted flowers that fiend for sunshine
During Greek times, the ladies lived fearfully
At the legality of being dismissed
Therefore becoming his submissive servant
Serving obediently, catering to her husband's slightest command
His laws made her property of man
Allowing him to take ownership of all her belongings and the

Products of her work
You see he hurt and debased the image of his mate
Shape'n the culture we live in today
Leading way, to the present way
In which the Black Man now treats his Queen

Mistreating his Queen by being
Disrespectful
Degrading the very nature of the Mother
See brother, I am the doorway through which
All creation has come
And where I'm from
"No nation can rise higher than its woman"
So coming at me with anything less
Will surely corrode our compatibility

Now unfortunately his fable was able to infect our minds
But we can no longer remain blind nor
Act unaware
That there aren't deceitful connotations
Alongside his eager participation
With the dissemination of Black music
Financing lyrics that deface and dislocate
Our sistahs
With the intention of imaging us as whores
For our brothers will never see us more than that
If we keep distastefully exposing our
Fat assess
Making them wobble wobble and
Shaky shake
Making money is more important than elevating your born mate?
Sistahs we can't ignore our imbedded trait and role
In being the first teacher of every human being
And seeing that the first impression is always lasting
We can't keep acting like
Exposing our children to low-natured musical concepts and
Disrespectful relationships with
Spoiled men made useless
Thinking just having one is for the best

Is all meaningless
These actions only perpetuate his mess
Not to mention the added stress

It's our natural mission to raise our children into mental maturity
Walking round like Little Kim wannabes
Not respecting me
Is not your full capability
Thinking you've done done something
Because you've slept with my boyfriend...
On da low
Forgetting that he's just a man
So that shit ain't hard to do
Nor is being a hoe
Yourself you need to check
In order to gain respect from our brothers
We have to respect each other
For we are the Mothers of Civilization

Respect me/Let thee/Guide we/Infinitely
Treat me/Kindly/Making we/Come to be

Now my dear sweet brothers
I understand that there has been an
Indescribable pain
Inflicted upon your manhood, over and over again
The demeaning relationships
Not to mention the shit
Ya own mama put you through
However, Boo
We can't delete your past
So the designated task I know you must perform now
In order to heal we
Is to defeat your Ego
Recondition your mind and
Protect me

Protect me from false images on TV
Lyrics used to degrade me
Fulfill your role to protect and provide

For we can no longer hide nor run from change
Prearranged to our birth
Is the certainty of growth

Respect the Mother
Protect us Brother
For there is no other route to
Life and liberty
But through we
The Woman
The Mother
The Magick!

Inspired by the Creator expressed through
Merlin Stone's "When God Was A Woman"

Parent/Child

Now this madness has got to stop
This smothering
Hovering
Lifelong power struggling
Mechanically steering children of God to become
Possessions of man
I am not a possession of man
I am a Spirit
Light and free
Born to live purposely
Fulfilling my divine purpose
So, why you projecting YOUR desires on me?
When they haven't fully satisfied you
And maybe, just maybe...that's not what I want to do!
And yes I may have come through you
But I am not yours and
You don't own me

The role you've been given is to instill in me
All that I need to make proper choices in life
That will bring me prosperity, peace, and love
But all you do is force and shove your
Conditioned thoughts
Down my throat
Forcing me to think, live, and act in a way
In which you believe I should be
Your method isn't any different from what is called
"Slavery"

As you unconsciously fill me with stale tales and
Overlooked fears that you've been fed
And when I finally see where they have led you
And desire not to journey along that path
You lash out at me with painful condemning words
Contradicting what I just heard you say
"Judge not that ye be not judged"
Isn't that the Christ way?

So if I decide to sway along a road that's different from
The one you have chosen

Why am I chastised and convicted?
Why is my free will constantly taken away with
Ill punishments and anger-filled whippings
When I probably just repeated what I saw you do
But yet you can do and say whatever you want to
And your actions are disregarded as "sin"
Because you the "Parent" and I'm the "Child"
I love you dearly "Parent"
But your theory sounds pretty ig'nant and wild
And so very far from the truth
Don't be a fool to think that "Karma"
Gone skip over you
Because it ain't
And parenting ain't meant to last throughout one's
Entire life
How can one be an adult but...still "yo" child?
This style of parenting, is making children resentful
Thus, we have to become mindful and realize that
At a certain point one must let go and
Allow the bird to fly
Allowing one to be
Yes, you are my physical Mom and Dad
Given the task to guide and nurture me
From my higher Mother/Father Creator
The All-Knowing
The Almighty
Thus, I am not yours and you don't own me
We are all spirits born equally
So maybe if you start looking at the
Role of a "Parent", as such
The present state of our society wouldn't be in a crutch
We would be living much more
Harmoniously

And so every time you fuss at me
Telling me what I should be doing and
That I'm not living right or
Don't talk to you like that cuz...you the mama
Ignoring the fact that I am a grown azz woman
Regardless if I live at home with you or not

Your power struggles only create a lot of
Unnecessary drama
Now words can't express how much we love
Momma and Dad
But nevertheless, you're still holding on to something that
Isn't meant to be held on to
Now this doesn't mean that one does not appreciate you
And all that you do and have done
But just because we are your sons and daughters
Doesn't mean that we don't equate
And just because you've been here more years, this lifetime
Than I
Doesn't conclusively mean that
You are more wise
For wisdom comes by learning lessons
Thus, I can develop by learning from your mistakes
That you may unconsciously make a thousand times

This poem is not meant to be "disrespectful"
For it is only that I find
Our present state of parenting
No longer producing liberation
But only creating binds
Thus it is time to revise and revolutionize
This poem was written to open eyes and to
Awaken souls
So we can start making those vital changes
In order for our seeds to have that
Peace of mind
We've been struggling to get and have not yet gotten
We want our seeds to evolve, not to rotten
We must let go of old ideals and old patterns
Changing our perceptions
Changing our thoughts
To the new and to the bold
So our lives can unfold into what
God has created them to be
And she has created them to be
Great!

I am aware that it takes
Courage and spiritual understanding
To even swallow these words that I've expressed
So I can only hope and pray that you open your heart and
Let them blossom within
Let's take this Parent/Child relationship to
A higher level
And start relating as equals and spiritual Friends

We We

I don't understand a word
That is coming out of yo' mouth
Cuz me no speak'a Ingles
Any mo'
Y yo no habla Espanola
Meaning — I can't discern a word you saying bro
El French la la
Is the only language I recognize
So if you can't verbalize it
Just let me be
Cuz this sistah refuse to listen to I, I, I any longer
It's all about
We We

You see I's selfish azz
Never attempts to give or compromise
While WE always trying to
Make the situation pleasing for both
And so WE patiently waits and hopes that
You'd let go of those self-centered plots that you
Unconsciously plan
Inevitably causing shit to hit the fan
Cuz you keep failing to understand that
Two heads is always better than one
So until WE come togetha
Our prosperity will never get betta
Nor grow expeditiously
Because I moves more slowly than WE
So what YOU need to do is
Get ya mind right
And start accepting me and my role
You gots to fight this mind control
Cuz it's diggin us into deeper holes
Not only spiritually and mentally
But economically
For it is WE that makes bank balances rise
Faster than I trying to do it on its own
The time that it takes I to do what WE can
Could be spent on devising a plan
In healing our communities

So that WE don't have to worry about
Corruption
Taking what WE have worked so hard to get
Plus, these repetitive ego trips of
I not needing anyone to get ahead
I can do it on its own
Is starting to get on my
Got damn nerves
Because it took more than just sperm
To get you here
Is my language clear?
Because yours ain't

Can't you see that this I mentality
Has changed society
To one lacking humanity that
WE would never create
I has terrorized
Murdered lives
All in the name of Peace
Using War as its tool
I is an ignorant fool
For not recognizing after all these centuries of
Massive pains and sufferings that
Maybe it should start handling things a little differently?
Like stepping back and allowing WE to rule again
I is not developed enough to lead our nations
Nor our homes
Because I condones
Jealously, envy, anger, and hate
I is the culprit that creates an imbalance in wealth
Where you have one group of people
Poor, starving, and lacking health
And then the other living in excess
I's politics is scandalous
For WE have to make a comeback
Our present condition reveals the fact that
I ain't doing the job

So before I attempts to fully rob WE
Of its humanity
Let me reiterate and make sure that this is heard

I don't understand a word
That is coming out of yo' mouth
Cuz me no speak'a Ingles
Any mo'
Y yo no habla Espanola
Meaning — I can't discern a word you saying bro
El French la la
Is the only language I recognize
So if you can't verbalize it
Just let me be
Cuz this sistah refuse to listen to I, I, I any longer
It's all about

We We

Bring Ya Azz! ───────────────────

It feels like I haven't spoken to you in months
I didn't realize how strong my feelings
Are
For you
And yes I'm speaking in the present tense
Because presently I sense
A feeling that someone very very special
Is absent in my life

It feels like I haven't spoken to you in years
I didn't realize how intense
The energies amongst us
Were
Shared
And yeah I'm speaking of those yesterdays
That felt like eternity
Whenever we
Infrequently
Joined together
In space and time
Whenever we briefly delved into the depths of our minds
Whenever our bodies occasionally intertwined in
Warm cuddles or those
Hot love makings

Though we seldomly shared the same space
Because e-mail took the place
Yet, our few experiences were so great
And so profound that
It feels like I haven't spoken to you in ages
I didn't realize what you
Mean
In my life
And yeah I'm speaking again of the present
Moment
In which
I desire
You to be
Actively participating in mine
And I in your
Life

Damn!
Why you had to go and act trifling
Making things more complicated than need be
When all you had to do was be honest with me
So very simple but
Why so hard for many?

As you ignored the many times I forgave and
Forgot
And I know that the latter is so very rare
But how can you not bear witness to
The fact that no matter, I refused to place judgment on you
Regardless of what you did or do
And so whatever your truth
It could've been spoken
So there was no need to feed me deception
There was no need for you to play games
My love for you will not change
My love for you wants to grow
It wants to evolve into
An energy source as powerful as
Our Sun
Healing bodies
Radiating light onto all
Radiating light onto our
Great, great, great grandkids
That are sure to come
As soon as you get it togetha
So I can open up and give you some
For I am eagerly anticipating
The moment we make up and
Re-begin
This time with Truth, Harmony, and Justice as our
Matrons of Honors
Balance, Order, and Righteousness
For Groomsmen

And I know that when I quantify the period
That we have not spoken
It has only been one month and a day

That feels like eternity
And this eternity has brought me to fully realize
That you are someone very special
Who means so very much
In my life
Past, present, and future
So would you
Get ya shit togetha and
Bring ya azz!

For we have a lot of important things to make happen
In this lifetime

I Challenge You ———————————

Brotha you don't have to flex
I can see your bulging muscles from here

I can see your thick azz neck
And arms that can no longer rest by your waist side

I've peeped your defined thighs and
Wide heavy fists
Which definitely send out a message that
You ain't to be messed with
For your physical strength is too great

However, I would now like to take this time to
See what "real" strength you have
Because nowadays the size of one's physique
Is a thing of the past
With all these man-made guns and
Nuclear weapons
A fist now holds no weight in teaching lessons
So how about testing your muscles on
Higher ground
And let's see how profound your strength really is
Let's see if you really are
"The Man"
Let's see what you really can do
So Brotha Man, I now challenge you

I challenge you in your ability to rid yourself of
Lies
And the infamous Ego
So I can experience the God hidden beneath

I challenge you to defeat your
Need to control
Possess and
Be on top
So I can sop you up like a biscuit
With my healing tongue and pleasing mouth

I challenge you to re-route down

An entirely new path
One that leads to your higher self
But this path would require help from
Me
It would require that you'd become vulnerable to
Little ole, non having any muscles
Me
And the obstacles along it can only be won
If at all times I am treated as a
Queen

Now this doesn't mean that you'd have to become
Weaker
And I would be taking away your powers
It would simply show that you are not
A slave to
The mind
And your ability to change it
Would clearly display
That it is your servant
And not ruler of your higher spirit

So I challenge you to take this path
And let's see how long you can last
Will you solve the math?
Solve the equation?
Uncover your truth
Let's see how far your mental and spiritual muscles
Will take you

Will you believe yourself to be weak?
Stop and turn back?
Or will you doubt and question not your strength and abilities?
And continue moving forward?
Overcoming all obstacles
Reaching your center

Brotha Man, I now challenge you to enter into
My womb
I challenge you to enter into it

133

In openness, vulnerability, and
Trust
It is a must that you submit to my
Wisdom
And with this bravery you shall become wise
God-like
Master of this material realm
A place of being
That only a few have attempted to reach
And have attained
Which can only be gained through me
So I now challenge you

Do you accept?

Take It Baby

Take it baby
Take it
It is yours
It has always been
They have just made you to forget
By filling you with
Insecurities
Superficialities
False realities
Struggles of being a man
Struggles of surviving
Providing
Protecting
Been plotting to keep you guessing about
Who and what you are
God
You beautiful Black Man you

So take it baby
Take it
It is yours
It has always been
But you just have been, stuck on some
Fearfulness
Afraid to grab hold of it
By the horns
Afraid of becoming who and what you are
God
You beautiful Black Man you

Take it
Take your throne
You better take it like you own, something
Because you do
It is your birthright
So take it
Take seat of your rightful throne
Positioned right beside mine
Because a sistah been sitting alone now
For quite some time

And so now is the time for you to

Take it
Take this royal love
My royal blood
That I've been trying to give
Hers was made for his
So take it baby
Take it
It is yours
It is all of yours to delve within and
Rejuvenate
I am your
Perfectly Divine Mate
My dear sweet prince who still hesitates
In becoming a King
Thus, entering into
The Kingdom of God
My Heaven

So take it
Take me baby
I am yours
What are you waiting for?
Aren't you ready to explore
Heaven
Right here on Earth
So take it baby
I won't hurt you
I only want to take you
Into Heaven
With me
So take me
I am yours

Take it
Take yours

About the Author

A native of Detroit, Kamilah Hasan is a woman of many talents and insights. She attended Cass Technical High School, one of the top high schools in Detroit, which prepared her for academic studies at Michigan State University where she received a Bachelors of Arts Degree in Accounting. During the period she attended the University she began delving into her creative side that opened the door for the expression of her poetry as well as other art forms. Kamilah has graced the stage as a dancer and actress as well as poetess. "A Taste of My Forehead and Backside" is a cumulative work of her life experiences, dreams, and spirit's work thus far. Ms. Hasan has an extraordinary outlook on the seen and unseen universe taking her viewers, listeners, and readers to new levels of understanding, perceiving, and experiencing life. Her poetry explores all facets of the human experience through colorful images created by vivid word play. She exudes the essence of a Royal Queen Mother, a magician, a spiritual warrior, and just plain ole "Milah."

Peace & light on your journey—-

Tene' L. Dismuke-Beaver
Friend and soul sistah

About the Illustrator

Jevon Dismuke is an artist with multidimensional talent. This young artist has been creating images all his life. He brings the unconscious into view through his illustrations and designs, showing the world an eccentric perception on normal images. A former student of Kendall Art and Design and Saci in Florence Italy, Jevon has acquired a vast amount of technique in the visual arts with meticulous attention to detail and aesthetic. He is proficient in various mediums such as ink, charcoal, watercolor, acrylic, oil, graphite, printmaking, and silk-screening and mix media. Jevon is inspired by the style of the Masters but brings an urban intuition and flair to everything he touches.

Tene' L. Dismuke
Sister & mentor